Security Architectures Complete Self-Assessment Guide

The guidance in this Self-Assessment is based on Security Architectures best practices and standards in business process architecture, design and quality management. The guidance is also based on the professional judgment of the individual collaborators listed in the Acknowledgments.

Table of Contents

About The Art of Service

The Art of Service, Business Process Architects since 2000, is dedicated to helping stakeholders achieve excellence.

Defining, designing, creating, and implementing a process to solve a stakeholders challenge or meet an objective is the most valuable role... In EVERY group, company, organization and department.

Unless you're talking a one-time, single-use project, there should be a process. Whether that process is managed and implemented by humans, AI, or a combination of the two, it needs to be designed by someone with a complex enough perspective to ask the right questions.

Someone capable of asking the right questions and step back and say, 'What are we really trying to accomplish here? And is there a different way to look at it?'

With The Art of Service's Standard Requirements Self-Assessments, we empower people who can do just that — whether their title is marketer, entrepreneur, manager, salesperson, consultant, Business Process Manager, executive assistant, IT Manager, CIO etc... —they are the people who rule the future. They are people who watch the process as it happens, and ask the right questions to make the process work better.

Contact us when you need any support with this Self-Assessment and any help with templates, blue-prints and examples of standard documents you might need:

http://theartofservice.com
service@theartofservice.com

Acknowledgments

This checklist was developed under the auspices of The Art of Service, chaired by Gerardus Blokdyk.

Representatives from several client companies participated in the preparation of this Self-Assessment.

In addition, we are thankful for the design and printing services provided.

Included Resources - how to access

Included with your purchase of the book is the Security Architectures Self-Assessment Spreadsheet Dashboard which contains all questions and Self-Assessment areas and auto-generates insights, graphs, and project RACI planning - all with examples to get you started right away.

How? Simply send an email to
access@theartofservice.com
with this books' title in the subject to get the Security Architectures Self Assessment Tool right away.

You will receive the following contents with New and Updated specific criteria:

- The latest quick edition of the book in PDF
- The latest complete edition of the book in PDF, which criteria correspond to the criteria in...
- The Self-Assessment Excel Dashboard, and...
- Example pre-filled Self-Assessment Excel Dashboard to get familiar with results generation
- In-depth specific Checklists covering the topic
- Project management checklists and templates to assist with implementation

INCLUDES LIFETIME SELF ASSESSMENT UPDATES

Every self assessment comes with Lifetime Updates and Lifetime Free Updated Books. Lifetime Updates is an industry-first feature which allows you to receive verified self assessment updates, ensuring you always have the most accurate information at your fingertips.

Get it now- you will be glad you did - do it now, before you forget.

Send an email to **access@theartofservice.com** with this books' title in the subject to get the Security Architectures Self Assessment Tool right away.

Your feedback is invaluable to us

If you recently bought this book, we would love to hear from you! You can do this by writing a review on amazon (or the online store where you purchased this book) about your last purchase! As part of our continual service improvement process, we love to hear real client experiences and feedback.

How does it work?
To post a review on Amazon, just log in to your account and click on the Create Your Own Review button (under Customer Reviews) of the relevant product page. You can find examples of product reviews in Amazon. If you purchased from another online store, simply follow their procedures.

What happens when I submit my review?
Once you have submitted your review, send us an email at review@theartofservice.com with the link to your review so we can properly thank you for your feedback.

Purpose of this Self-Assessment

This Self-Assessment has been developed to improve understanding of the requirements and elements of Security Architectures, based on best practices and standards in business process architecture, design and quality management.

It is designed to allow for a rapid Self-Assessment to determine how closely existing management practices and procedures correspond to the elements of the Self-Assessment.

The criteria of requirements and elements of Security Architectures have been rephrased in the format of a Self-Assessment questionnaire, with a seven-criterion scoring system, as explained in this document.

In this format, even with limited background knowledge of

Security Architectures, a manager can quickly review existing operations to determine how they measure up to the standards. This in turn can serve as the starting point of a 'gap analysis' to identify management tools or system elements that might usefully be implemented in the organization to help improve overall performance.

How to use the Self-Assessment

On the following pages are a series of questions to identify to what extent your Security Architectures initiative is complete in comparison to the requirements set in standards.

To facilitate answering the questions, there is a space in front of each question to enter a score on a scale of '1' to '5'.

1 Strongly Disagree

2 Disagree

3 Neutral

4 Agree

5 Strongly Agree

Read the question and rate it with the following in front of mind:

'In my belief,
the answer to this question is clearly defined'.

There are two ways in which you can choose to interpret this statement;

1. how aware are you that the answer to the question is clearly defined
2. for more in-depth analysis you can choose to gather

evidence and confirm the answer to the question. This obviously will take more time, most Self-Assessment users opt for the first way to interpret the question and dig deeper later on based on the outcome of the overall Self-Assessment.

A score of '1' would mean that the answer is not clear at all, where a '5' would mean the answer is crystal clear and defined. Leave emtpy when the question is not applicable or you don't want to answer it, you can skip it without affecting your score. Write your score in the space provided.

After you have responded to all the appropriate statements in each section, compute your average score for that section, using the formula provided, and round to the nearest tenth. Then transfer to the corresponding spoke in the Security Architectures Scorecard on the second next page of the Self-Assessment.

Your completed Security Architectures Scorecard will give you a clear presentation of which Security Architectures areas need attention.

Security Architectures Scorecard Example

Example of how the finalized Scorecard can look like:

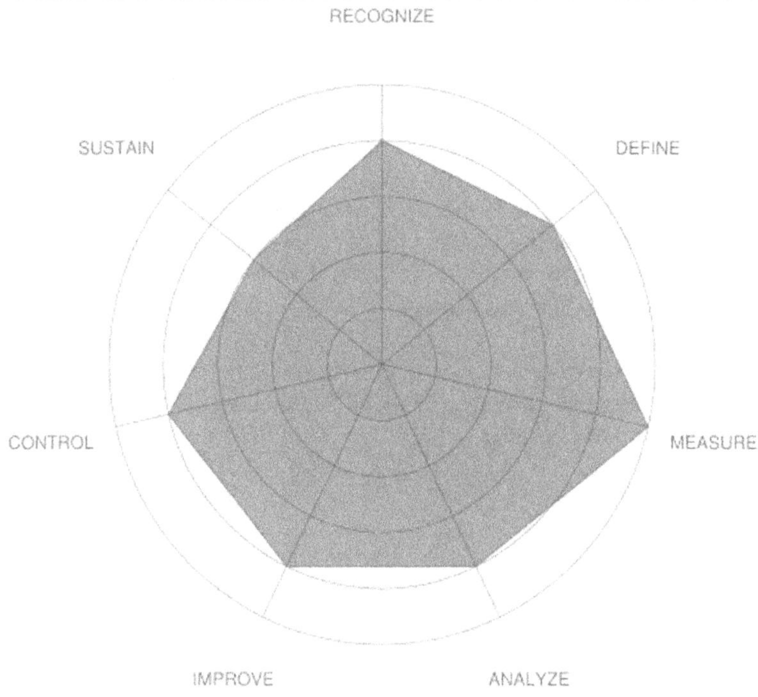

Security Architectures Scorecard

Your Scores:

BEGINNING OF THE SELF-ASSESSMENT:

CRITERION #1: RECOGNIZE

INTENT: Be aware of the need for change. Recognize that there is an unfavorable variation, problem or symptom.

In my belief, the answer to this question is clearly defined:

5 Strongly Agree

4 Agree

3 Neutral

2 Disagree

1 Strongly Disagree

1. What extra resources will you need?
<--- Score

2. To what extent does each concerned units management team recognize Security Architectures as an effective investment?
<--- Score

3. Can management personnel recognize the

monetary benefit of Security Architectures?
<--- Score

4. Are there regulatory / compliance issues?
<--- Score

5. What is the problem and/or vulnerability?
<--- Score

6. What are the minority interests and what amount of minority interests can be recognized?
<--- Score

7. How do you identify the kinds of information that you will need?
<--- Score

8. To what extent would your organization benefit from being recognized as a award recipient?
<--- Score

9. Would you recognize a threat from the inside?
<--- Score

10. Are employees recognized or rewarded for performance that demonstrates the highest levels of integrity?
<--- Score

11. Who are your key stakeholders who need to sign off?
<--- Score

12. Is the need for organizational change recognized?
<--- Score

13. Do you need to avoid or amend any Security Architectures activities?
<--- Score

14. What else needs to be measured?
<--- Score

15. Is it needed?
<--- Score

16. How much are sponsors, customers, partners, stakeholders involved in Security Architectures? In other words, what are the risks, if Security Architectures does not deliver successfully?
<--- Score

17. Will a response program recognize when a crisis occurs and provide some level of response?
<--- Score

18. What are the expected benefits of Security Architectures to the stakeholder?
<--- Score

19. Why is this needed?
<--- Score

20. What is the problem or issue?
<--- Score

21. What creative shifts do you need to take?
<--- Score

22. Is it clear when you think of the day ahead of you what activities and tasks you need to complete?
<--- Score

23. How does it fit into your organizational needs and tasks?
<--- Score

24. What situation(s) led to this Security Architectures Self Assessment?
<--- Score

25. What are the Security Architectures resources needed?
<--- Score

26. Where do you need to exercise leadership?
<--- Score

27. Is the quality assurance team identified?
<--- Score

28. What Security Architectures capabilities do you need?
<--- Score

29. What is the smallest subset of the problem you can usefully solve?
<--- Score

30. How do you take a forward-looking perspective in identifying Security Architectures research related to market response and models?
<--- Score

31. Why the need?
<--- Score

32. Are your goals realistic? Do you need to redefine

your problem? Perhaps the problem has changed or maybe you have reached your goal and need to set a new one?
<--- Score

33. Think about the people you identified for your Security Architectures project and the project responsibilities you would assign to them, what kind of training do you think they would need to perform these responsibilities effectively?
<--- Score

34. Does Security Architectures create potential expectations in other areas that need to be recognized and considered?
<--- Score

35. Looking at each person individually – does every one have the qualities which are needed to work in this group?
<--- Score

36. Are losses recognized in a timely manner?
<--- Score

37. How do you recognize an objection?
<--- Score

38. What should be considered when identifying available resources, constraints, and deadlines?
<--- Score

39. Who needs to know?
<--- Score

40. Which information does the Security Architectures

business case need to include?
<--- Score

41. As a sponsor, customer or management, how important is it to meet goals, objectives?
<--- Score

42. What problems are you facing and how do you consider Security Architectures will circumvent those obstacles?
<--- Score

43. What needs to stay?
<--- Score

44. Do you know what you need to know about Security Architectures?
<--- Score

45. Are there any specific expectations or concerns about the Security Architectures team, Security Architectures itself?
<--- Score

46. Are employees recognized for desired behaviors?
<--- Score

47. Do you recognize Security Architectures achievements?
<--- Score

48. Are you dealing with any of the same issues today as yesterday? What can you do about this?
<--- Score

49. Who needs budgets?

<--- Score

50. Who needs what information?
<--- Score

51. Are controls defined to recognize and contain problems?
<--- Score

52. What vendors make products that address the Security Architectures needs?
<--- Score

53. What training and capacity building actions are needed to implement proposed reforms?
<--- Score

54. What resources or support might you need?
<--- Score

55. How many trainings, in total, are needed?
<--- Score

56. What information do users need?
<--- Score

57. Does the problem have ethical dimensions?
<--- Score

58. What Security Architectures problem should be solved?
<--- Score

59. Who else hopes to benefit from it?
<--- Score

60. What Security Architectures events should you attend?
<--- Score

61. Are there Security Architectures problems defined?
<--- Score

62. Which needs are not included or involved?
<--- Score

63. How do you recognize an Security Architectures objection?
<--- Score

64. Are there recognized Security Architectures problems?
<--- Score

65. Do you have/need 24-hour access to key personnel?
<--- Score

66. Where is training needed?
<--- Score

67. How are you going to measure success?
<--- Score

68. Consider your own Security Architectures project, what types of organizational problems do you think might be causing or affecting your problem, based on the work done so far?
<--- Score

69. Does your organization need more Security

Architectures education?
<--- Score

70. What activities does the governance board need to consider?
<--- Score

71. Are problem definition and motivation clearly presented?
<--- Score

72. Have you identified your Security Architectures key performance indicators?
<--- Score

73. What do you need to start doing?
<--- Score

74. How can auditing be a preventative security measure?
<--- Score

75. Who should resolve the Security Architectures issues?
<--- Score

76. What prevents you from making the changes you know will make you a more effective Security Architectures leader?
<--- Score

77. What are the clients issues and concerns?
<--- Score

78. What does Security Architectures success mean to the stakeholders?

<--- Score

79. For your Security Architectures project, identify and describe the business environment, is there more than one layer to the business environment?
<--- Score

80. What Security Architectures coordination do you need?
<--- Score

81. How do you identify subcontractor relationships?
<--- Score

82. What needs to be done?
<--- Score

83. Are there any revenue recognition issues?
<--- Score

84. What is the Security Architectures problem definition? What do you need to resolve?
<--- Score

85. What do employees need in the short term?
<--- Score

86. Did you miss any major Security Architectures issues?
<--- Score

87. Who defines the rules in relation to any given issue?
<--- Score

88. Will it solve real problems?
<--- Score

89. What is the recognized need?
<--- Score

90. Who needs to know about Security Architectures?
<--- Score

91. How are training requirements identified?
<--- Score

92. What would happen if Security Architectures weren't done?
<--- Score

93. How are the Security Architectures's objectives aligned to the group's overall stakeholder strategy?
<--- Score

94. What are the timeframes required to resolve each of the issues/problems?
<--- Score

95. What are your needs in relation to Security Architectures skills, labor, equipment, and markets?
<--- Score

96. Will new equipment/products be required to facilitate Security Architectures delivery, for example is new software needed?
<--- Score

97. Which issues are too important to ignore?
<--- Score

98. Will Security Architectures deliverables need to be tested and, if so, by whom?
<--- Score

99. What are the stakeholder objectives to be achieved with Security Architectures?
<--- Score

Add up total points for this section:
_____ = Total points for this section

Divided by: ______ (number of statements answered) = ______ Average score for this section

Transfer your score to the Security Architectures Index at the beginning of the Self-Assessment.

CRITERION #2: DEFINE:

INTENT: Formulate the stakeholder problem. Define the problem, needs and objectives.

In my belief, the answer to this question is clearly defined:

5 Strongly Agree

4 Agree

3 Neutral

2 Disagree

1 Strongly Disagree

1. How will variation in the actual durations of each activity be dealt with to ensure that the expected Security Architectures results are met?
<--- Score

2. Is the team adequately staffed with the desired cross-functionality? If not, what additional resources are available to the team?
<--- Score

3. In what way can you redefine the criteria of choice clients have in your category in your favor?
<--- Score

4. What is the worst case scenario?
<--- Score

5. How do you manage changes in Security Architectures requirements?
<--- Score

6. How have you defined all Security Architectures requirements first?
<--- Score

7. What are the rough order estimates on cost savings/ opportunities that Security Architectures brings?
<--- Score

8. Are approval levels defined for contracts and supplements to contracts?
<--- Score

9. Has a team charter been developed and communicated?
<--- Score

10. Has your scope been defined?
<--- Score

11. What is out of scope?
<--- Score

12. What is the scope of the Security Architectures work?

<--- Score

13. How do you think the partners involved in Security Architectures would have defined success?
<--- Score

14. How would you define Security Architectures leadership?
<--- Score

15. What defines best in class?
<--- Score

16. Is the scope of Security Architectures defined?
<--- Score

17. What scope do you want your strategy to cover?
<--- Score

18. Is data collected and displayed to better understand customer(s) critical needs and requirements.
<--- Score

19. Is there a completed, verified, and validated high-level 'as is' (not 'should be' or 'could be') stakeholder process map?
<--- Score

20. What are the boundaries of the scope? What is in bounds and what is not? What is the start point? What is the stop point?
<--- Score

21. What scope to assess?

<--- Score

22. When is the estimated completion date?
<--- Score

23. What are the compelling stakeholder reasons for embarking on Security Architectures?
<--- Score

24. What are the Roles and Responsibilities for each team member and its leadership? Where is this documented?
<--- Score

25. How do you gather Security Architectures requirements?
<--- Score

26. Have all basic functions of Security Architectures been defined?
<--- Score

27. What are the Security Architectures use cases?
<--- Score

28. Scope of sensitive information?
<--- Score

29. How is the team tracking and documenting its work?
<--- Score

30. Are audit criteria, scope, frequency and methods defined?
<--- Score

31. What gets examined?
<--- Score

32. Are required metrics defined, what are they?
<--- Score

33. What information should you gather?
<--- Score

34. Is there regularly 100% attendance at the team meetings? If not, have appointed substitutes attended to preserve cross-functionality and full representation?
<--- Score

35. How often are the team meetings?
<--- Score

36. How does the Security Architectures manager ensure against scope creep?
<--- Score

37. Has the Security Architectures work been fairly and/or equitably divided and delegated among team members who are qualified and capable to perform the work? Has everyone contributed?
<--- Score

38. Do you all define Security Architectures in the same way?
<--- Score

39. What constraints exist that might impact the team?
<--- Score

40. Is the improvement team aware of the different versions of a process: what they think it is vs. what it actually is vs. what it should be vs. what it could be?
<--- Score

41. How do you catch Security Architectures definition inconsistencies?
<--- Score

42. Are there different segments of customers?
<--- Score

43. What customer feedback methods were used to solicit their input?
<--- Score

44. How will the Security Architectures team and the group measure complete success of Security Architectures?
<--- Score

45. How do you keep key subject matter experts in the loop?
<--- Score

46. Who is gathering information?
<--- Score

47. Does the team have regular meetings?
<--- Score

48. What Security Architectures requirements should be gathered?
<--- Score

49. How do you manage unclear Security

Architectures requirements?
<--- Score

50. Is Security Architectures linked to key stakeholder goals and objectives?
<--- Score

51. Are different versions of process maps needed to account for the different types of inputs?
<--- Score

52. Has the improvement team collected the 'voice of the customer' (obtained feedback – qualitative and quantitative)?
<--- Score

53. Has anyone else (internal or external to the group) attempted to solve this problem or a similar one before? If so, what knowledge can be leveraged from these previous efforts?
<--- Score

54. What are the core elements of the Security Architectures business case?
<--- Score

55. What are the tasks and definitions?
<--- Score

56. Have the customer needs been translated into specific, measurable requirements? How?
<--- Score

57. Who is gathering Security Architectures information?
<--- Score

58. What are (control) requirements for Security Architectures Information?
<--- Score

59. Are the Security Architectures requirements complete?
<--- Score

60. How and when will the baselines be defined?
<--- Score

61. What are the Security Architectures tasks and definitions?
<--- Score

62. Is there any additional Security Architectures definition of success?
<--- Score

63. What specifically is the problem? Where does it occur? When does it occur? What is its extent?
<--- Score

64. Is the current 'as is' process being followed? If not, what are the discrepancies?
<--- Score

65. Who are the Security Architectures improvement team members, including Management Leads and Coaches?
<--- Score

66. Have all of the relationships been defined properly?
<--- Score

67. Are the Security Architectures requirements testable?
<--- Score

68. What baselines are required to be defined and managed?
<--- Score

69. Is there a critical path to deliver Security Architectures results?
<--- Score

70. What is in scope?
<--- Score

71. How can the value of Security Architectures be defined?
<--- Score

72. Has everyone on the team, including the team leaders, been properly trained?
<--- Score

73. How was the 'as is' process map developed, reviewed, verified and validated?
<--- Score

74. Has the direction changed at all during the course of Security Architectures? If so, when did it change and why?
<--- Score

75. What Security Architectures services do you require?
<--- Score

76. What is the definition of Security Architectures excellence?
<--- Score

77. Why are you doing Security Architectures and what is the scope?
<--- Score

78. What is the definition of success?
<--- Score

79. Will a Security Architectures production readiness review be required?
<--- Score

80. Is the Security Architectures scope manageable?
<--- Score

81. Is Security Architectures currently on schedule according to the plan?
<--- Score

82. What system do you use for gathering Security Architectures information?
<--- Score

83. Is there a Security Architectures management charter, including stakeholder case, problem and goal statements, scope, milestones, roles and responsibilities, communication plan?
<--- Score

84. Is there a completed SIPOC representation, describing the Suppliers, Inputs, Process, Outputs, and Customers?

<--- Score

85. What is in the scope and what is not in scope?
<--- Score

86. What is a worst-case scenario for losses?
<--- Score

87. What key stakeholder process output measure(s) does Security Architectures leverage and how?
<--- Score

88. Has a Security Architectures requirement not been met?
<--- Score

89. Do the problem and goal statements meet the SMART criteria (specific, measurable, attainable, relevant, and time-bound)?
<--- Score

90. What sort of initial information to gather?
<--- Score

91. What is the scope of Security Architectures?
<--- Score

92. What information do you gather?
<--- Score

93. What intelligence can you gather?
<--- Score

94. What are the requirements for audit information?
<--- Score

95. How did the Security Architectures manager receive input to the development of a Security Architectures improvement plan and the estimated completion dates/times of each activity?
<--- Score

96. Is it clearly defined in and to your organization what you do?
<--- Score

97. How do you gather the stories?
<--- Score

98. What are the dynamics of the communication plan?
<--- Score

99. How do you gather requirements?
<--- Score

100. Do you have organizational privacy requirements?
<--- Score

101. What is the scope of the Security Architectures effort?
<--- Score

102. If substitutes have been appointed, have they been briefed on the Security Architectures goals and received regular communications as to the progress to date?
<--- Score

103. Is special Security Architectures user knowledge required?

<--- Score

104. Are all requirements met?
<--- Score

105. How do you hand over Security Architectures context?
<--- Score

106. Are resources adequate for the scope?
<--- Score

107. When is/was the Security Architectures start date?
<--- Score

108. When are meeting minutes sent out? Who is on the distribution list?
<--- Score

109. What is the scope?
<--- Score

110. Has a high-level 'as is' process map been completed, verified and validated?
<--- Score

111. What would be the goal or target for a Security Architectures's improvement team?
<--- Score

112. Has/have the customer(s) been identified?
<--- Score

113. Is scope creep really all bad news?
<--- Score

114. Has a project plan, Gantt chart, or similar been developed/completed?
<--- Score

115. Where can you gather more information?
<--- Score

116. Who defines (or who defined) the rules and roles?
<--- Score

117. Are there any constraints known that bear on the ability to perform Security Architectures work? How is the team addressing them?
<--- Score

118. Do you have a Security Architectures success story or case study ready to tell and share?
<--- Score

119. What critical content must be communicated – who, what, when, where, and how?
<--- Score

120. What was the context?
<--- Score

121. How do you build the right business case?
<--- Score

122. The political context: who holds power?
<--- Score

123. What are the record-keeping requirements of Security Architectures activities?
<--- Score

124. Who approved the Security Architectures scope?
<--- Score

125. Are accountability and ownership for Security Architectures clearly defined?
<--- Score

126. How are consistent Security Architectures definitions important?
<--- Score

127. Is Security Architectures required?
<--- Score

128. Have specific policy objectives been defined?
<--- Score

129. Are task requirements clearly defined?
<--- Score

130. Is there a clear Security Architectures case definition?
<--- Score

Add up total points for this section:
_____ = Total points for this section

Divided by: ______ (number of statements answered) = ______
Average score for this section

Transfer your score to the Security Architectures Index at the beginning of the Self-Assessment.

CRITERION #3: MEASURE:

INTENT: Gather the correct data. Measure the current performance and evolution of the situation.

In my belief, the answer to this question is clearly defined:

5 Strongly Agree

4 Agree

3 Neutral

2 Disagree

1 Strongly Disagree

1. Was a life-cycle cost analysis performed?
<--- Score

2. What is the cause of any Security Architectures gaps?
<--- Score

3. What does losing customers cost your organization?
<--- Score

4. What causes investor action?
<--- Score

5. Among the Security Architectures product and service cost to be estimated, which is considered hardest to estimate?
<--- Score

6. How do you verify and validate the Security Architectures data?
<--- Score

7. Which costs should be taken into account?
<--- Score

8. When are costs are incurred?
<--- Score

9. What are your customers expectations and measures?
<--- Score

10. Was a business case (cost/benefit) developed?
<--- Score

11. Are there competing Security Architectures priorities?
<--- Score

12. How do you verify the authenticity of the data and information used?
<--- Score

13. How is performance measured?
<--- Score

14. What is the root cause(s) of the problem?
<--- Score

15. How do you measure lifecycle phases?
<--- Score

16. How is progress measured?
<--- Score

17. What is the total fixed cost?
<--- Score

18. What are the uncertainties surrounding estimates of impact?
<--- Score

19. Does a Security Architectures quantification method exist?
<--- Score

20. How will effects be measured?
<--- Score

21. How sensitive must the Security Architectures strategy be to cost?
<--- Score

22. What could cause delays in the schedule?
<--- Score

23. What are the strategic priorities for this year?
<--- Score

24. Are the measurements objective?
<--- Score

25. When should you bother with diagrams?
<--- Score

26. Which measures and indicators matter?
<--- Score

27. The approach of traditional Security Architectures works for detail complexity but is focused on a systematic approach rather than an understanding of the nature of systems themselves, what approach will permit your organization to deal with the kind of unpredictable emergent behaviors that dynamic complexity can introduce?
<--- Score

28. What are predictive Security Architectures analytics?
<--- Score

29. What are the estimated costs of proposed changes?
<--- Score

30. What measurements are being captured?
<--- Score

31. What do people want to verify?
<--- Score

32. Is a follow-up focused external Security Architectures review required?
<--- Score

33. What is your Security Architectures quality cost segregation study?

<--- Score

34. Are Security Architectures vulnerabilities categorized and prioritized?
<--- Score

35. What relevant entities could be measured?
<--- Score

36. What does verifying compliance entail?
<--- Score

37. What kind of analytics data will be gathered?
<--- Score

38. What are your primary costs, revenues, assets?
<--- Score

39. What are the current costs of the Security Architectures process?
<--- Score

40. Do you verify that corrective actions were taken?
<--- Score

41. What could cause you to change course?
<--- Score

42. How can you manage cost down?
<--- Score

43. How will measures be used to manage and adapt?
<--- Score

44. How are costs allocated?

<--- Score

45. How will your organization measure success?
<--- Score

46. What are the Security Architectures investment costs?
<--- Score

47. How do you measure success?
<--- Score

48. How are measurements made?
<--- Score

49. What are the costs and benefits?
<--- Score

50. How do you verify and develop ideas and innovations?
<--- Score

51. What harm might be caused?
<--- Score

52. How do you verify performance?
<--- Score

53. Are there measurements based on task performance?
<--- Score

54. How do you measure efficient delivery of Security Architectures services?
<--- Score

55. How do you stay flexible and focused to recognize larger Security Architectures results?
<--- Score

56. Are there any easy-to-implement alternatives to Security Architectures? Sometimes other solutions are available that do not require the cost implications of a full-blown project?
<--- Score

57. Is there an opportunity to verify requirements?
<--- Score

58. How frequently do you track Security Architectures measures?
<--- Score

59. Do you have a flow diagram of what happens?
<--- Score

60. Is the solution cost-effective?
<--- Score

61. How do you focus on what is right -not who is right?
<--- Score

62. How will you measure success?
<--- Score

63. What are hidden Security Architectures quality costs?
<--- Score

64. Where is it measured?
<--- Score

65. How do you aggregate measures across priorities?
<--- Score

66. Is the cost worth the Security Architectures effort ?
<--- Score

67. How do you verify if Security Architectures is built right?
<--- Score

68. At what cost?
<--- Score

69. Have design-to-cost goals been established?
<--- Score

70. What happens if cost savings do not materialize?
<--- Score

71. Does the Security Architectures task fit the client's priorities?
<--- Score

72. How are you verifying it?
<--- Score

73. How do you measure variability?
<--- Score

74. Which Security Architectures impacts are significant?
<--- Score

75. What are the costs of delaying Security Architectures action?
<--- Score

76. How to cause the change?
<--- Score

77. Is it possible to estimate the impact of unanticipated complexity such as wrong or failed assumptions, feedback, etcetera on proposed reforms?
<--- Score

78. Are actual costs in line with budgeted costs?
<--- Score

79. How do you verify the Security Architectures requirements quality?
<--- Score

80. Do you aggressively reward and promote the people who have the biggest impact on creating excellent Security Architectures services/products?
<--- Score

81. Do the benefits outweigh the costs?
<--- Score

82. What does your operating model cost?
<--- Score

83. Will Security Architectures have an impact on current business continuity, disaster recovery processes and/or infrastructure?
<--- Score

84. Where can you go to verify the info?
<--- Score

85. How will the Security Architectures data be analyzed?
<--- Score

86. Have you made assumptions about the shape of the future, particularly its impact on your customers and competitors?
<--- Score

87. When a disaster occurs, who gets priority?
<--- Score

88. Why do the measurements/indicators matter?
<--- Score

89. What are the Security Architectures key cost drivers?
<--- Score

90. Are you taking your company in the direction of better and revenue or cheaper and cost?
<--- Score

91. What is your cost benefit analysis?
<--- Score

92. Who should receive measurement reports?
<--- Score

93. How do you quantify and qualify impacts?
<--- Score

94. What are your operating costs?

<--- Score

95. What tests verify requirements?
<--- Score

96. How can you reduce costs?
<--- Score

97. How is the value delivered by Security Architectures being measured?
<--- Score

98. Are missed Security Architectures opportunities costing your organization money?
<--- Score

99. How can you reduce the costs of obtaining inputs?
<--- Score

100. What is measured? Why?
<--- Score

101. Where is the cost?
<--- Score

102. How will costs be allocated?
<--- Score

103. How can you measure Security Architectures in a systematic way?
<--- Score

104. Are supply costs steady or fluctuating?
<--- Score

105. What can be used to verify compliance?
<--- Score

106. Are you able to realize any cost savings?
<--- Score

107. What would be a real cause for concern?
<--- Score

108. What are allowable costs?
<--- Score

109. Are the units of measure consistent?
<--- Score

110. Do you have an issue in getting priority?
<--- Score

111. What would it cost to replace your technology?
<--- Score

112. What are you verifying?
<--- Score

113. How will you measure your Security Architectures effectiveness?
<--- Score

114. Who is involved in verifying compliance?
<--- Score

115. What are the costs of reform?
<--- Score

116. What are the types and number of measures to use?

<--- Score

117. What do you measure and why?
<--- Score

118. How does cost-to-serve analysis help?
<--- Score

119. Are indirect costs charged to the Security Architectures program?
<--- Score

120. How can a Security Architectures test verify your ideas or assumptions?
<--- Score

121. What causes extra work or rework?
<--- Score

122. What evidence is there and what is measured?
<--- Score

123. How do you control the overall costs of your work processes?
<--- Score

124. How do you verify Security Architectures completeness and accuracy?
<--- Score

125. Is the scope of Security Architectures cost analysis cost-effective?
<--- Score

126. What details are required of the Security Architectures cost structure?

<--- Score

127. What does a Test Case verify?
<--- Score

128. How do your measurements capture actionable Security Architectures information for use in exceeding your customers expectations and securing your customers engagement?
<--- Score

129. What measurements are possible, practicable and meaningful?
<--- Score

130. How do you verify your resources?
<--- Score

131. What causes innovation to fail or succeed in your organization?
<--- Score

132. What is the cost of rework?
<--- Score

133. Have you included everything in your Security Architectures cost models?
<--- Score

134. What drives O&M cost?
<--- Score

135. What are the costs?
<--- Score

136. Are the Security Architectures benefits worth

its costs?
<--- Score

137. Who pays the cost?
<--- Score

138. What causes mismanagement?
<--- Score

139. How much does it cost?
<--- Score

140. What disadvantage does this cause for the user?
<--- Score

141. Has a cost center been established?
<--- Score

Add up total points for this section:
_____ = Total points for this section

Divided by: ______ (number of statements answered) = ______ Average score for this section

Transfer your score to the Security Architectures Index at the beginning of the Self-Assessment.

CRITERION #4: ANALYZE:

INTENT: Analyze causes, assumptions and hypotheses.

In my belief, the answer to this question is clearly defined:

5 Strongly Agree

4 Agree

3 Neutral

2 Disagree

1 Strongly Disagree

1. Do your leaders quickly bounce back from setbacks?
<--- Score

2. Where can you get qualified talent today?
<--- Score

3. Is data and process analysis, root cause analysis and quantifying the gap/opportunity in place?
<--- Score

4. Was a detailed process map created to amplify critical steps of the 'as is' stakeholder process?
<--- Score

5. What methods do you use to gather Security Architectures data?
<--- Score

6. What process improvements will be needed?
<--- Score

7. What is the Value Stream Mapping?
<--- Score

8. Has an output goal been set?
<--- Score

9. What tools were used to generate the list of possible causes?
<--- Score

10. What is the Security Architectures Driver?
<--- Score

11. Have any additional benefits been identified that will result from closing all or most of the gaps?
<--- Score

12. Have you defined which data is gathered how?
<--- Score

13. Who owns what data?
<--- Score

14. Is pre-qualification of suppliers carried out?

<--- Score

15. Where is the data coming from to measure compliance?
<--- Score

16. What is the cost of poor quality as supported by the team's analysis?
<--- Score

17. What qualifications are necessary?
<--- Score

18. What are the necessary qualifications?
<--- Score

19. What data do you need to collect?
<--- Score

20. What are your key performance measures or indicators and in-process measures for the control and improvement of your Security Architectures processes?
<--- Score

21. Who gets your output?
<--- Score

22. How is the data gathered?
<--- Score

23. What is your organizations process which leads to recognition of value generation?
<--- Score

24. How was the detailed process map generated,

verified, and validated?
<--- Score

25. What are the revised rough estimates of the financial savings/opportunity for Security Architectures improvements?
<--- Score

26. What conclusions were drawn from the team's data collection and analysis? How did the team reach these conclusions?
<--- Score

27. What kind of crime could a potential new hire have committed that would not only not disqualify him/her from being hired by your organization, but would actually indicate that he/she might be a particularly good fit?
<--- Score

28. How do your work systems and key work processes relate to and capitalize on your core competencies?
<--- Score

29. How do mission and objectives affect the Security Architectures processes of your organization?
<--- Score

30. What qualifications do Security Architectures leaders need?
<--- Score

31. What other jobs or tasks affect the performance of the steps in the Security Architectures process?

<--- Score

32. How are outputs preserved and protected?
<--- Score

33. What are the Security Architectures business drivers?
<--- Score

34. How do you define collaboration and team output?
<--- Score

35. How do you promote understanding that opportunity for improvement is not criticism of the status quo, or the people who created the status quo?
<--- Score

36. What are evaluation criteria for the output?
<--- Score

37. Is the Security Architectures process severely broken such that a re-design is necessary?
<--- Score

38. Do your employees have the opportunity to do what they do best everyday?
<--- Score

39. Were any designed experiments used to generate additional insight into the data analysis?
<--- Score

40. What Security Architectures data do you gather or use now?
<--- Score

41. What quality tools were used to get through the analyze phase?
<--- Score

42. Was a cause-and-effect diagram used to explore the different types of causes (or sources of variation)?
<--- Score

43. What qualifies as competition?
<--- Score

44. How do you use Security Architectures data and information to support organizational decision making and innovation?
<--- Score

45. How will the Security Architectures data be captured?
<--- Score

46. Were Pareto charts (or similar) used to portray the 'heavy hitters' (or key sources of variation)?
<--- Score

47. How is the way you as the leader think and process information affecting your organizational culture?
<--- Score

48. What do you need to qualify?
<--- Score

49. What other organizational variables, such as reward systems or communication systems, affect the performance of this Security Architectures process?

<--- Score

50. Think about the functions involved in your Security Architectures project, what processes flow from these functions?
<--- Score

51. Is the gap/opportunity displayed and communicated in financial terms?
<--- Score

52. How does the organization define, manage, and improve its Security Architectures processes?
<--- Score

53. Has data output been validated?
<--- Score

54. What are your outputs?
<--- Score

55. Is there an established change management process?
<--- Score

56. How is Security Architectures data gathered?
<--- Score

57. Do staff qualifications match your project?
<--- Score

58. A compounding model resolution with available relevant data can often provide insight towards a solution methodology; which Security Architectures models, tools and techniques are necessary?
<--- Score

59. Who is involved with workflow mapping?
<--- Score

60. What is your organizations system for selecting qualified vendors?
<--- Score

61. What are your best practices for minimizing Security Architectures project risk, while demonstrating incremental value and quick wins throughout the Security Architectures project lifecycle?
<--- Score

62. Have the problem and goal statements been updated to reflect the additional knowledge gained from the analyze phase?
<--- Score

63. What types of data do your Security Architectures indicators require?
<--- Score

64. Who qualifies to gain access to data?
<--- Score

65. What are your current levels and trends in key Security Architectures measures or indicators of product and process performance that are important to and directly serve your customers?
<--- Score

66. What will drive Security Architectures change?
<--- Score

67. How difficult is it to qualify what Security Architectures ROI is?
<--- Score

68. What did the team gain from developing a sub-process map?
<--- Score

69. What tools were used to narrow the list of possible causes?
<--- Score

70. Do you, as a leader, bounce back quickly from setbacks?
<--- Score

71. Where is Security Architectures data gathered?
<--- Score

72. Do your contracts/agreements contain data security obligations?
<--- Score

73. Do you understand your management processes today?
<--- Score

74. How many input/output points does it require?
<--- Score

75. An organizationally feasible system request is one that considers the mission, goals and objectives of the organization, key questions are: is the Security Architectures solution request practical and will it solve a problem or take advantage of an opportunity to achieve company goals?

<--- Score

76. Are all staff in core Security Architectures subjects Highly Qualified?
<--- Score

77. What process should you select for improvement?
<--- Score

78. Did any value-added analysis or 'lean thinking' take place to identify some of the gaps shown on the 'as is' process map?
<--- Score

79. Are you missing Security Architectures opportunities?
<--- Score

80. How do you measure the operational performance of your key work systems and processes, including productivity, cycle time, and other appropriate measures of process effectiveness, efficiency, and innovation?
<--- Score

81. Which Security Architectures data should be retained?
<--- Score

82. What internal processes need improvement?
<--- Score

83. Are gaps between current performance and the goal performance identified?
<--- Score

84. What data is gathered?
<--- Score

85. What are the personnel training and qualifications required?
<--- Score

86. What is the output?
<--- Score

87. What is the oversight process?
<--- Score

88. What information qualified as important?
<--- Score

89. How do you ensure that the Security Architectures opportunity is realistic?
<--- Score

90. Are all team members qualified for all tasks?
<--- Score

91. What, related to, Security Architectures processes does your organization outsource?
<--- Score

92. What resources go in to get the desired output?
<--- Score

93. Do quality systems drive continuous improvement?
<--- Score

94. What are the disruptive Security Architectures technologies that enable your organization to

radically change your business processes?
<--- Score

95. How is the Security Architectures Value Stream Mapping managed?
<--- Score

96. Do you have the authority to produce the output?
<--- Score

97. How much data can be collected in the given timeframe?
<--- Score

98. What training and qualifications will you need?
<--- Score

99. What were the financial benefits resulting from any 'ground fruit or low-hanging fruit' (quick fixes)?
<--- Score

100. What does the data say about the performance of the stakeholder process?
<--- Score

101. Who will gather what data?
<--- Score

102. Can you add value to the current Security Architectures decision-making process (largely qualitative) by incorporating uncertainty modeling (more quantitative)?
<--- Score

103. How do you identify specific Security

Architectures investment opportunities and emerging trends?
<--- Score

104. Is the suppliers process defined and controlled?
<--- Score

105. What are your current levels and trends in key measures or indicators of Security Architectures product and process performance that are important to and directly serve your customers? How do these results compare with the performance of your competitors and other organizations with similar offerings?
<--- Score

106. How will the change process be managed?
<--- Score

107. What controls do you have in place to protect data?
<--- Score

108. Did any additional data need to be collected?
<--- Score

109. Is the required Security Architectures data gathered?
<--- Score

110. Do several people in different organizational units assist with the Security Architectures process?
<--- Score

111. Is the final output clearly identified?

<--- Score

112. Is the performance gap determined?
<--- Score

113. How can risk management be tied procedurally to process elements?
<--- Score

114. Who is involved in the management review process?
<--- Score

115. What Security Architectures metrics are outputs of the process?
<--- Score

116. How do you implement and manage your work processes to ensure that they meet design requirements?
<--- Score

117. What output to create?
<--- Score

118. What qualifications and skills do you need?
<--- Score

119. Think about some of the processes you undertake within your organization, which do you own?
<--- Score

120. What were the crucial 'moments of truth' on the process map?
<--- Score

121. How often will data be collected for measures?
<--- Score

122. Is there a strict change management process?
<--- Score

123. Are your outputs consistent?
<--- Score

124. What successful thing are you doing today that may be blinding you to new growth opportunities?
<--- Score

125. Were there any improvement opportunities identified from the process analysis?
<--- Score

Add up total points for this section:
_____ = Total points for this section

Divided by: ______ (number of statements answered) = ______ Average score for this section

Transfer your score to the Security Architectures Index at the beginning of the Self-Assessment.

CRITERION #5: IMPROVE:

INTENT: Develop a practical solution. Innovate, establish and test the solution and to measure the results.

In my belief, the answer to this question is clearly defined:

5 Strongly Agree

4 Agree

3 Neutral

2 Disagree

1 Strongly Disagree

1. Who controls key decisions that will be made?
<--- Score

2. How can you better manage risk?
<--- Score

3. If you could go back in time five years, what decision would you make differently? What is your best guess as to what decision you're making

today you might regret five years from now?
<--- Score

4. How will you measure the results?
<--- Score

5. What is the implementation plan?
<--- Score

6. How do you mitigate Security Architectures risk?
<--- Score

7. What criteria will you use to assess your Security Architectures risks?
<--- Score

8. What are the affordable Security Architectures risks?
<--- Score

9. What were the underlying assumptions on the cost-benefit analysis?
<--- Score

10. How do you improve productivity?
<--- Score

11. How risky is your organization?
<--- Score

12. Is the solution technically practical?
<--- Score

13. Is there a high likelihood that any recommendations will achieve their intended results?
<--- Score

14. Who controls the risk?
<--- Score

15. Was a Security Architectures charter developed?
<--- Score

16. Is the optimal solution selected based on testing and analysis?
<--- Score

17. How significant is the improvement in the eyes of the end user?
<--- Score

18. How does the solution remove the key sources of issues discovered in the analyze phase?
<--- Score

19. Would you develop a Security Architectures Communication Strategy?
<--- Score

20. Are risk triggers captured?
<--- Score

21. Do you combine technical expertise with business knowledge and Security Architectures Key topics include lifecycles, development approaches, requirements and how to make a business case?
<--- Score

22. What were the criteria for evaluating a Security Architectures pilot?
<--- Score

23. Who will be using the results of the measurement activities?
<--- Score

24. Have you identified breakpoints and/or risk tolerances that will trigger broad consideration of a potential need for intervention or modification of strategy?
<--- Score

25. How do you measure progress and evaluate training effectiveness?
<--- Score

26. How do you manage Security Architectures risk?
<--- Score

27. How can the phases of Security Architectures development be identified?
<--- Score

28. At what point will vulnerability assessments be performed once Security Architectures is put into production (e.g., ongoing Risk Management after implementation)?
<--- Score

29. Who are the key stakeholders for the Security Architectures evaluation?
<--- Score

30. How do you improve your likelihood of success ?
<--- Score

31. Risk events: what are the things that could go wrong?

<--- Score

32. Is pilot data collected and analyzed?
<--- Score

33. For decision problems, how do you develop a decision statement?
<--- Score

34. Who should make the Security Architectures decisions?
<--- Score

35. What lessons, if any, from a pilot were incorporated into the design of the full-scale solution?
<--- Score

36. How are Security Architectures risks managed?
<--- Score

37. What is the magnitude of the improvements?
<--- Score

38. Is a solution implementation plan established, including schedule/work breakdown structure, resources, risk management plan, cost/budget, and control plan?
<--- Score

39. What is Security Architectures's impact on utilizing the best solution(s)?
<--- Score

40. Will the controls trigger any other risks?
<--- Score

41. Explorations of the frontiers of Security Architectures will help you build influence, improve Security Architectures, optimize decision making, and sustain change, what is your approach?
<--- Score

42. Which Security Architectures solution is appropriate?
<--- Score

43. To what extent does management recognize Security Architectures as a tool to increase the results?
<--- Score

44. What can you do to improve?
<--- Score

45. What should a proof of concept or pilot accomplish?
<--- Score

46. What to do with the results or outcomes of measurements?
<--- Score

47. How do you improve Security Architectures service perception, and satisfaction?
<--- Score

48. Is the Security Architectures documentation thorough?
<--- Score

49. How can you improve Security Architectures?
<--- Score

50. How will you recognize and celebrate results?
<--- Score

51. What attendant changes will need to be made to ensure that the solution is successful?
<--- Score

52. How will the group know that the solution worked?
<--- Score

53. Describe the design of the pilot and what tests were conducted, if any?
<--- Score

54. Can the solution be designed and implemented within an acceptable time period?
<--- Score

55. Does a good decision guarantee a good outcome?
<--- Score

56. Is any Security Architectures documentation required?
<--- Score

57. How does your organization evaluate strategic Security Architectures success?
<--- Score

58. What improvements have been achieved?
<--- Score

59. What does the 'should be' process map/design look like?

<--- Score

60. Risk factors: what are the characteristics of Security Architectures that make it risky?
<--- Score

61. Do you need to do a usability evaluation?
<--- Score

62. What are the expected Security Architectures results?
<--- Score

63. What error proofing will be done to address some of the discrepancies observed in the 'as is' process?
<--- Score

64. Is the scope clearly documented?
<--- Score

65. In the past few months, what is the smallest change you have made that has had the biggest positive result? What was it about that small change that produced the large return?
<--- Score

66. What is the Security Architectures's sustainability risk?
<--- Score

67. Is the Security Architectures risk managed?
<--- Score

68. How do you link measurement and risk?
<--- Score

69. How do you manage and improve your Security Architectures work systems to deliver customer value and achieve organizational success and sustainability?
<--- Score

70. How are policy decisions made and where?
<--- Score

71. What are the concrete Security Architectures results?
<--- Score

72. Are there any constraints (technical, political, cultural, or otherwise) that would inhibit certain solutions?
<--- Score

73. Where do the Security Architectures decisions reside?
<--- Score

74. Is there a small-scale pilot for proposed improvement(s)? What conclusions were drawn from the outcomes of a pilot?
<--- Score

75. What tools were used to tap into the creativity and encourage 'outside the box' thinking?
<--- Score

76. Is a contingency plan established?
<--- Score

77. What went well, what should change, what can improve?
<--- Score

78. Have you achieved Security Architectures improvements?
<--- Score

79. Are decisions made in a timely manner?
<--- Score

80. How do you define the solutions' scope?
<--- Score

81. How scalable is your Security Architectures solution?
<--- Score

82. Risk Identification: What are the possible risk events your organization faces in relation to Security Architectures?
<--- Score

83. What are the implications of the one critical Security Architectures decision 10 minutes, 10 months, and 10 years from now?
<--- Score

84. What area needs the greatest improvement?
<--- Score

85. How will you know that you have improved?
<--- Score

86. What risks do you need to manage?
<--- Score

87. How do the Security Architectures results compare with the performance of your competitors and other

organizations with similar offerings?
<--- Score

88. Is risk periodically assessed?
<--- Score

89. Is there a cost/benefit analysis of optimal solution(s)?
<--- Score

90. Does the goal represent a desired result that can be measured?
<--- Score

91. What is the team's contingency plan for potential problems occurring in implementation?
<--- Score

92. How can skill-level changes improve Security Architectures?
<--- Score

93. For estimation problems, how do you develop an estimation statement?
<--- Score

94. Who makes the Security Architectures decisions in your organization?
<--- Score

95. How do you go about comparing Security Architectures approaches/solutions?
<--- Score

96. Were any criteria developed to assist the team in testing and evaluating potential solutions?

<--- Score

97. What are your current levels and trends in key measures or indicators of workforce and leader development?
<--- Score

98. Who will be responsible for documenting the Security Architectures requirements in detail?
<--- Score

99. Security Architectures risk decisions: whose call Is It?
<--- Score

100. What tools were most useful during the improve phase?
<--- Score

101. Is the measure of success for Security Architectures understandable to a variety of people?
<--- Score

102. Was a pilot designed for the proposed solution(s)?
<--- Score

103. Are you assessing Security Architectures and risk?
<--- Score

104. What do you want to improve?
<--- Score

105. What communications are necessary to support the implementation of the solution?
<--- Score

106. Are events managed to resolution?
<--- Score

107. What strategies for Security Architectures improvement are successful?
<--- Score

108. How will the team or the process owner(s) monitor the implementation plan to see that it is working as intended?
<--- Score

109. How risky is your organization?
<--- Score

110. Where do you need Security Architectures improvement?
<--- Score

111. Who will be responsible for making the decisions to include or exclude requested changes once Security Architectures is underway?
<--- Score

112. Do you cover the five essential competencies: Communication, Collaboration,Innovation, Adaptability, and Leadership that improve an organizations ability to leverage the new Security Architectures in a volatile global economy?
<--- Score

113. How did the team generate the list of possible solutions?
<--- Score

114. How will you know when its improved?
<--- Score

115. What Security Architectures improvements can be made?
<--- Score

116. When you map the key players in your own work and the types/domains of relationships with them, which relationships do you find easy and which challenging, and why?
<--- Score

117. What tools were used to evaluate the potential solutions?
<--- Score

118. Which of the recognised risks out of all risks can be most likely transferred?
<--- Score

119. Who are the people involved in developing and implementing Security Architectures?
<--- Score

120. Who do you report Security Architectures results to?
<--- Score

121. What resources are required for the improvement efforts?
<--- Score

122. How do you measure risk?
<--- Score

123. What needs improvement? Why?
<--- Score

124. What practices helps your organization to develop its capacity to recognize patterns?
<--- Score

125. What actually has to improve and by how much?
<--- Score

126. Is the implementation plan designed?
<--- Score

127. How will you know that a change is an improvement?
<--- Score

128. Are the best solutions selected?
<--- Score

129. Can you identify any significant risks or exposures to Security Architectures third- parties (vendors, service providers, alliance partners etc) that concern you?
<--- Score

130. Do vendor agreements bring new compliance risk ?
<--- Score

131. How do you deal with Security Architectures risk?
<--- Score

132. How can you improve performance?
<--- Score

133. Is supporting Security Architectures documentation required?
<--- Score

134. Why improve in the first place?
<--- Score

135. Who manages Security Architectures risk?
<--- Score

136. How does the team improve its work?
<--- Score

137. What is the risk?
<--- Score

Add up total points for this section:
_____ = Total points for this section

Divided by: ______ (number of statements answered) = ______ Average score for this section

Transfer your score to the Security Architectures Index at the beginning of the Self-Assessment.

CRITERION #6: CONTROL:

INTENT: Implement the practical solution. Maintain the performance and correct possible complications.

In my belief, the answer to this question is clearly defined:

5 Strongly Agree

4 Agree

3 Neutral

2 Disagree

1 Strongly Disagree

1. What Security Architectures standards are applicable?
<--- Score

2. Who will be in control?
<--- Score

3. How do you plan on providing proper recognition and disclosure of supporting

companies?
<--- Score

4. Where do ideas that reach policy makers and planners as proposals for Security Architectures strengthening and reform actually originate?
<--- Score

5. Has the improved process and its steps been standardized?
<--- Score

6. Does the Security Architectures performance meet the customer's requirements?
<--- Score

7. Who controls critical resources?
<--- Score

8. How will the process owner and team be able to hold the gains?
<--- Score

9. What should the next improvement project be that is related to Security Architectures?
<--- Score

10. Do the Security Architectures decisions you make today help people and the planet tomorrow?
<--- Score

11. How do your controls stack up?
<--- Score

12. What other areas of the group might benefit from the Security Architectures team's improvements,

knowledge, and learning?
<--- Score

13. What is the best design framework for Security Architectures organization now that, in a post industrial-age if the top-down, command and control model is no longer relevant?
<--- Score

14. Are controls in place and consistently applied?
<--- Score

15. Does job training on the documented procedures need to be part of the process team's education and training?
<--- Score

16. Are the planned controls working?
<--- Score

17. Has the Security Architectures value of standards been quantified?
<--- Score

18. Is knowledge gained on process shared and institutionalized?
<--- Score

19. Are new process steps, standards, and documentation ingrained into normal operations?
<--- Score

20. Are the planned controls in place?
<--- Score

21. What is the control/monitoring plan?

<--- Score

22. Who is going to spread your message?
<--- Score

23. Against what alternative is success being measured?
<--- Score

24. Are pertinent alerts monitored, analyzed and distributed to appropriate personnel?
<--- Score

25. Are the Security Architectures standards challenging?
<--- Score

26. Are there documented procedures?
<--- Score

27. Will the team be available to assist members in planning investigations?
<--- Score

28. Is there a Security Architectures Communication plan covering who needs to get what information when?
<--- Score

29. Does the response plan contain a definite closed loop continual improvement scheme (e.g., plan-do-check-act)?
<--- Score

30. How is change control managed?
<--- Score

31. Are operating procedures consistent?
<--- Score

32. Who has control over resources?
<--- Score

33. How do controls support value?
<--- Score

34. How will new or emerging customer needs/requirements be checked/communicated to orient the process toward meeting the new specifications and continually reducing variation?
<--- Score

35. What adjustments to the strategies are needed?
<--- Score

36. How might the group capture best practices and lessons learned so as to leverage improvements?
<--- Score

37. Are you measuring, monitoring and predicting Security Architectures activities to optimize operations and profitability, and enhancing outcomes?
<--- Score

38. What should you measure to verify efficiency gains?
<--- Score

39. What key inputs and outputs are being measured on an ongoing basis?

<--- Score

40. What are your results for key measures or indicators of the accomplishment of your Security Architectures strategy and action plans, including building and strengthening core competencies?
<--- Score

41. What are the critical parameters to watch?
<--- Score

42. You may have created your quality measures at a time when you lacked resources, technology wasn't up to the required standard, or low service levels were the industry norm. Have those circumstances changed?
<--- Score

43. Is there a control plan in place for sustaining improvements (short and long-term)?
<--- Score

44. How will report readings be checked to effectively monitor performance?
<--- Score

45. Does Security Architectures appropriately measure and monitor risk?
<--- Score

46. How will input, process, and output variables be checked to detect for sub-optimal conditions?
<--- Score

47. What is your theory of human motivation, and how does your compensation plan fit with that view?

<--- Score

48. Is new knowledge gained imbedded in the response plan?
<--- Score

49. Is there a documented and implemented monitoring plan?
<--- Score

50. Will existing staff require re-training, for example, to learn new business processes?
<--- Score

51. How likely is the current Security Architectures plan to come in on schedule or on budget?
<--- Score

52. How will you measure your QA plan's effectiveness?
<--- Score

53. What are the key elements of your Security Architectures performance improvement system, including your evaluation, organizational learning, and innovation processes?
<--- Score

54. Does a troubleshooting guide exist or is it needed?
<--- Score

55. How do senior leaders actions reflect a commitment to the organizations Security Architectures values?
<--- Score

56. How do you spread information?
<--- Score

57. Is there a standardized process?
<--- Score

58. How is Security Architectures project cost planned, managed, monitored?
<--- Score

59. Who sets the Security Architectures standards?
<--- Score

60. What do you measure to verify effectiveness gains?
<--- Score

61. Do you monitor the effectiveness of your Security Architectures activities?
<--- Score

62. How do you plan for the cost of succession?
<--- Score

63. What quality tools were useful in the control phase?
<--- Score

64. Are documented procedures clear and easy to follow for the operators?
<--- Score

65. What are you attempting to measure/monitor?
<--- Score

66. Is the Security Architectures test/monitoring

cost justified?
<--- Score

67. Are suggested corrective/restorative actions indicated on the response plan for known causes to problems that might surface?
<--- Score

68. Is there a recommended audit plan for routine surveillance inspections of Security Architectures's gains?
<--- Score

69. How do you select, collect, align, and integrate Security Architectures data and information for tracking daily operations and overall organizational performance, including progress relative to strategic objectives and action plans?
<--- Score

70. Is there a transfer of ownership and knowledge to process owner and process team tasked with the responsibilities.
<--- Score

71. How do you encourage people to take control and responsibility?
<--- Score

72. Have new or revised work instructions resulted?
<--- Score

73. How will the day-to-day responsibilities for monitoring and continual improvement be transferred from the improvement team to the process owner?

<--- Score

74. Will your goals reflect your program budget?
<--- Score

75. What do your reports reflect?
<--- Score

76. How will the process owner verify improvement in present and future sigma levels, process capabilities?
<--- Score

77. How do you establish and deploy modified action plans if circumstances require a shift in plans and rapid execution of new plans?
<--- Score

78. What do you stand for--and what are you against?
<--- Score

79. What other systems, operations, processes, and infrastructures (hiring practices, staffing, training, incentives/rewards, metrics/dashboards/scorecards, etc.) need updates, additions, changes, or deletions in order to facilitate knowledge transfer and improvements?
<--- Score

80. How will Security Architectures decisions be made and monitored?
<--- Score

81. What are customers monitoring?
<--- Score

82. Can you adapt and adjust to changing Security

Architectures situations?
<--- Score

83. What can you control?
<--- Score

84. What is the recommended frequency of auditing?
<--- Score

85. Is reporting being used or needed?
<--- Score

86. In the case of a Security Architectures project, the criteria for the audit derive from implementation objectives, an audit of a Security Architectures project involves assessing whether the recommendations outlined for implementation have been met, can you track that any Security Architectures project is implemented as planned, and is it working?
<--- Score

87. How widespread is its use?
<--- Score

88. Is a response plan established and deployed?
<--- Score

89. Will any special training be provided for results interpretation?
<--- Score

90. Is a response plan in place for when the input, process, or output measures indicate an 'out-of-control' condition?
<--- Score

91. Who is the Security Architectures process owner?
<--- Score

92. How can you best use all of your knowledge repositories to enhance learning and sharing?
<--- Score

93. Is there documentation that will support the successful operation of the improvement?
<--- Score

94. Implementation Planning: is a pilot needed to test the changes before a full roll out occurs?
<--- Score

95. What are the known security controls?
<--- Score

96. What is your plan to assess your security risks?
<--- Score

Add up total points for this section:
_____ = Total points for this section

Divided by: ______ (number of statements answered) = ______ Average score for this section

Transfer your score to the Security Architectures Index at the beginning of the Self-Assessment.

CRITERION #7: SUSTAIN:

INTENT: Retain the benefits.

In my belief, the answer to this question is clearly defined:

5 Strongly Agree

4 Agree

3 Neutral

2 Disagree

1 Strongly Disagree

1. How likely is it that a customer would recommend your company to a friend or colleague?
<--- Score

2. What is something you believe that nearly no one agrees with you on?
<--- Score

3. How do you stay inspired?
<--- Score

4. Which models, tools and techniques are necessary?
<--- Score

5. How do you manage Security Architectures Knowledge Management (KM)?
<--- Score

6. What have you done to protect your business from competitive encroachment?
<--- Score

7. Why will customers want to buy your organizations products/services?
<--- Score

8. Do you have the right capabilities and capacities?
<--- Score

9. What happens at your organization when people fail?
<--- Score

10. What are the success criteria that will indicate that Security Architectures objectives have been met and the benefits delivered?
<--- Score

11. Are you paying enough attention to the partners your company depends on to succeed?
<--- Score

12. Is Security Architectures dependent on the successful delivery of a current project?
<--- Score

13. Political -is anyone trying to undermine this

project?
<--- Score

14. What was the last experiment you ran?
<--- Score

15. How can you incorporate support to ensure safe and effective use of Security Architectures into the services that you provide?
<--- Score

16. What role does communication play in the success or failure of a Security Architectures project?
<--- Score

17. Who will provide the final approval of Security Architectures deliverables?
<--- Score

18. What is your question? Why?
<--- Score

19. Is the Security Architectures organization completing tasks effectively and efficiently?
<--- Score

20. What did you miss in the interview for the worst hire you ever made?
<--- Score

21. Who will determine interim and final deadlines?
<--- Score

22. What could happen if you do not do it?
<--- Score

23. Did your employees make progress today?
<--- Score

24. Why do and why don't your customers like your organization?
<--- Score

25. How do you set Security Architectures stretch targets and how do you get people to not only participate in setting these stretch targets but also that they strive to achieve these?
<--- Score

26. Who is responsible for Security Architectures?
<--- Score

27. How do you determine the key elements that affect Security Architectures workforce satisfaction, how are these elements determined for different workforce groups and segments?
<--- Score

28. Is Security Architectures realistic, or are you setting yourself up for failure?
<--- Score

29. Do you feel that more should be done in the Security Architectures area?
<--- Score

30. How do you create buy-in?
<--- Score

31. Who are the key stakeholders?
<--- Score

32. What is the kind of project structure that would be appropriate for your Security Architectures project, should it be formal and complex, or can it be less formal and relatively simple?
<--- Score

33. How do you track customer value, profitability or financial return, organizational success, and sustainability?
<--- Score

34. Where can you break convention?
<--- Score

35. Operational - will it work?
<--- Score

36. Who do you want your customers to become?
<--- Score

37. If you got fired and a new hire took your place, what would she do different?
<--- Score

38. Marketing budgets are tighter, consumers are more skeptical, and social media has changed forever the way we talk about Security Architectures, how do you gain traction?
<--- Score

39. What is an unauthorized commitment?
<--- Score

40. What are the challenges?
<--- Score

41. What is the overall talent health of your organization as a whole at senior levels, and for each organization reporting to a member of the Senior Leadership Team?
<--- Score

42. What are you trying to prove to yourself, and how might it be hijacking your life and business success?
<--- Score

43. What have been your experiences in defining long range Security Architectures goals?
<--- Score

44. Can you maintain your growth without detracting from the factors that have contributed to your success?
<--- Score

45. Do you think you know, or do you know you know ?
<--- Score

46. How do you make it meaningful in connecting Security Architectures with what users do day-to-day?
<--- Score

47. Are there any activities that you can take off your to do list?
<--- Score

48. Why should people listen to you?
<--- Score

49. Why is it important to have senior management support for a Security Architectures project?
<--- Score

50. What are specific Security Architectures rules to follow?
<--- Score

51. What potential megatrends could make your business model obsolete?
<--- Score

52. Are assumptions made in Security Architectures stated explicitly?
<--- Score

53. What stupid rule would you most like to kill?
<--- Score

54. What information is critical to your organization that your executives are ignoring?
<--- Score

55. What is the recommended frequency of auditing?
<--- Score

56. Can the schedule be done in the given time?
<--- Score

57. Is there a work around that you can use?
<--- Score

58. What current systems have to be understood and/or changed?
<--- Score

59. How can you become the company that would put you out of business?
<--- Score

60. How do you deal with Security Architectures changes?
<--- Score

61. Do you know who is a friend or a foe?
<--- Score

62. Who else should you help?
<--- Score

63. What are you challenging?
<--- Score

64. Are you satisfied with your current role? If not, what is missing from it?
<--- Score

65. Do you see more potential in people than they do in themselves?
<--- Score

66. What Security Architectures skills are most important?
<--- Score

67. If you weren't already in this business, would you enter it today? And if not, what are you going to do about it?
<--- Score

68. What are strategies for increasing support and reducing opposition?

<--- Score

69. Is your strategy driving your strategy? Or is the way in which you allocate resources driving your strategy?
<--- Score

70. What does your signature ensure?
<--- Score

71. What is your Security Architectures strategy?
<--- Score

72. If there were zero limitations, what would you do differently?
<--- Score

73. What may be the consequences for the performance of an organization if all stakeholders are not consulted regarding Security Architectures?
<--- Score

74. How do you foster innovation?
<--- Score

75. What are the short and long-term Security Architectures goals?
<--- Score

76. How do you foster the skills, knowledge, talents, attributes, and characteristics you want to have?
<--- Score

77. What are your personal philosophies regarding

Security Architectures and how do they influence your work?
<--- Score

78. What business benefits will Security Architectures goals deliver if achieved?
<--- Score

79. What are internal and external Security Architectures relations?
<--- Score

80. Which functions and people interact with the supplier and or customer?
<--- Score

81. To whom do you add value?
<--- Score

82. Which individuals, teams or departments will be involved in Security Architectures?
<--- Score

83. What will be the consequences to the stakeholder (financial, reputation etc) if Security Architectures does not go ahead or fails to deliver the objectives?
<--- Score

84. Will there be any necessary staff changes (redundancies or new hires)?
<--- Score

85. If you had to leave your organization for a year and the only communication you could have with employees/colleagues was a single paragraph, what would you write?

<--- Score

86. Do you say no to customers for no reason?
<--- Score

87. Do you have past Security Architectures successes?
<--- Score

88. Are you changing as fast as the world around you?
<--- Score

89. Can you break it down?
<--- Score

90. What would you recommend your friend do if he/she were facing this dilemma?
<--- Score

91. Instead of going to current contacts for new ideas, what if you reconnected with dormant contacts--the people you used to know? If you were going reactivate a dormant tie, who would it be?
<--- Score

92. Is a Security Architectures team work effort in place?
<--- Score

93. Who are your customers?
<--- Score

94. How do you ensure that implementations of Security Architectures products are done in a way that ensures safety?

<--- Score

95. If your customer were your grandmother, would you tell her to buy what you're selling?
<--- Score

96. What new services of functionality will be implemented next with Security Architectures ?
<--- Score

97. How do you cross-sell and up-sell your Security Architectures success?
<--- Score

98. What are current Security Architectures paradigms?
<--- Score

99. If you do not follow, then how to lead?
<--- Score

100. What trophy do you want on your mantle?
<--- Score

101. What would have to be true for the option on the table to be the best possible choice?
<--- Score

102. How long will it take to change?
<--- Score

103. What are the top 3 things at the forefront of your Security Architectures agendas for the next 3 years?
<--- Score

104. How do you assess the Security Architectures

pitfalls that are inherent in implementing it?
<--- Score

105. Who is responsible for ensuring appropriate resources (time, people and money) are allocated to Security Architectures?
<--- Score

106. What you are going to do to affect the numbers?
<--- Score

107. Whom among your colleagues do you trust, and for what?
<--- Score

108. What is your formula for success in Security Architectures ?
<--- Score

109. Who do you think the world wants your organization to be?
<--- Score

110. If your company went out of business tomorrow, would anyone who doesn't get a paycheck here care?
<--- Score

111. What is the source of the strategies for Security Architectures strengthening and reform?
<--- Score

112. How important is Security Architectures to the user organizations mission?
<--- Score

113. Are the criteria for selecting

recommendations stated?
<--- Score

114. What must you excel at?
<--- Score

115. How do you transition from the baseline to the target?
<--- Score

116. Do you have the right people on the bus?
<--- Score

117. What relationships among Security Architectures trends do you perceive?
<--- Score

118. How do you keep records, of what?
<--- Score

119. How do you know if you are successful?
<--- Score

120. How will you know that the Security Architectures project has been successful?
<--- Score

121. What are the key enablers to make this Security Architectures move?
<--- Score

122. Do you know what you are doing? And who do you call if you don't?
<--- Score

123. Who is on the team?

<--- Score

124. Think of your Security Architectures project, what are the main functions?
<--- Score

125. How do you maintain Security Architectures's Integrity?
<--- Score

126. Are the assumptions believable and achievable?
<--- Score

127. How much does Security Architectures help?
<--- Score

128. What management system can you use to leverage the Security Architectures experience, ideas, and concerns of the people closest to the work to be done?
<--- Score

129. Which Security Architectures goals are the most important?
<--- Score

130. How will you motivate the stakeholders with the least vested interest?
<--- Score

131. Would you rather sell to knowledgeable and informed customers or to uninformed customers?
<--- Score

132. How do you engage the workforce, in addition to

satisfying them?
<--- Score

133. Who is responsible for errors?
<--- Score

134. How can you become more high-tech but still be high touch?
<--- Score

135. What are the gaps in your knowledge and experience?
<--- Score

136. What is the craziest thing you can do?
<--- Score

137. How can you negotiate Security Architectures successfully with a stubborn boss, an irate client, or a deceitful coworker?
<--- Score

138. Is it economical; do you have the time and money?
<--- Score

139. In the past year, what have you done (or could you have done) to increase the accurate perception of your company/brand as ethical and honest?
<--- Score

140. Is your basic point _____ or _____?
<--- Score

141. How much contingency will be available in the budget?

<--- Score

142. What projects are going on in the organization today, and what resources are those projects using from the resource pools?
<--- Score

143. What is the funding source for this project?
<--- Score

144. What is a feasible sequencing of reform initiatives over time?
<--- Score

145. What are the business goals Security Architectures is aiming to achieve?
<--- Score

146. What are your most important goals for the strategic Security Architectures objectives?
<--- Score

147. Who, on the executive team or the board, has spoken to a customer recently?
<--- Score

148. Has implementation been effective in reaching specified objectives so far?
<--- Score

149. What is your BATNA (best alternative to a negotiated agreement)?
<--- Score

150. How do you keep the momentum going?
<--- Score

151. In a project to restructure Security Architectures outcomes, which stakeholders would you involve?
<--- Score

152. Do you have enough freaky customers in your portfolio pushing you to the limit day in and day out?
<--- Score

153. At what moment would you think; Will I get fired?
<--- Score

154. Who have you, as a company, historically been when you've been at your best?
<--- Score

155. How do you govern and fulfill your societal responsibilities?
<--- Score

156. What Security Architectures modifications can you make work for you?
<--- Score

157. What are the rules and assumptions your industry operates under? What if the opposite were true?
<--- Score

158. What are the potential basics of Security Architectures fraud?
<--- Score

159. If you find that you havent accomplished one of the goals for one of the steps of the Security

Architectures strategy, what will you do to fix it?
<--- Score

160. Are you relevant? Will you be relevant five years from now? Ten?
<--- Score

161. How do you accomplish your long range Security Architectures goals?
<--- Score

162. How is implementation research currently incorporated into each of your goals?
<--- Score

163. What is the range of capabilities?
<--- Score

164. If no one would ever find out about your accomplishments, how would you lead differently?
<--- Score

165. Is a Security Architectures breakthrough on the horizon?
<--- Score

166. Are you making progress, and are you making progress as Security Architectures leaders?
<--- Score

167. Who do we want your customers to become?
<--- Score

168. What goals did you miss?
<--- Score

169. Why not do Security Architectures?
<--- Score

170. How do you proactively clarify deliverables and Security Architectures quality expectations?
<--- Score

171. Are you / should you be revolutionary or evolutionary?
<--- Score

172. What happens when a new employee joins the organization?
<--- Score

173. What counts that you are not counting?
<--- Score

174. When information truly is ubiquitous, when reach and connectivity are completely global, when computing resources are infinite, and when a whole new set of impossibilities are not only possible, but happening, what will that do to your business?
<--- Score

175. How do senior leaders deploy your organizations vision and values through your leadership system, to the workforce, to key suppliers and partners, and to customers and other stakeholders, as appropriate?
<--- Score

176. Who uses your product in ways you never expected?
<--- Score

177. What should you stop doing?
<--- Score

178. Whose voice (department, ethnic group, women, older workers, etc) might you have missed hearing from in your company, and how might you amplify this voice to create positive momentum for your business?
<--- Score

179. What is the purpose of Security Architectures in relation to the mission?
<--- Score

180. How do you lead with Security Architectures in mind?
<--- Score

181. Do you think Security Architectures accomplishes the goals you expect it to accomplish?
<--- Score

182. What is the overall business strategy?
<--- Score

183. How will you insure seamless interoperability of Security Architectures moving forward?
<--- Score

184. Do you have an implicit bias for capital investments over people investments?
<--- Score

185. Who is the main stakeholder, with ultimate responsibility for driving Security Architectures forward?

<--- Score

186. Why is Security Architectures important for you now?
<--- Score

187. Are you using a design thinking approach and integrating Innovation, Security Architectures Experience, and Brand Value?
<--- Score

188. What one word do you want to own in the minds of your customers, employees, and partners?
<--- Score

189. Are you maintaining a past–present–future perspective throughout the Security Architectures discussion?
<--- Score

190. Are all key stakeholders present at all Structured Walkthroughs?
<--- Score

191. What unique value proposition (UVP) do you offer?
<--- Score

192. Ask yourself: how would you do this work if you only had one staff member to do it?
<--- Score

193. How will you ensure you get what you expected?
<--- Score

194. How are you doing compared to your industry?
<--- Score

195. How do customers see your organization?
<--- Score

196. How do you listen to customers to obtain actionable information?
<--- Score

197. What are the essentials of internal Security Architectures management?
<--- Score

198. Who will manage the integration of tools?
<--- Score

199. What are the long-term Security Architectures goals?
<--- Score

200. Is there any existing Security Architectures governance structure?
<--- Score

201. What is effective Security Architectures?
<--- Score

202. What is your competitive advantage?
<--- Score

203. If you were responsible for initiating and implementing major changes in your organization, what steps might you take to ensure acceptance of those changes?
<--- Score

204. What knowledge, skills and characteristics mark a good Security Architectures project manager?
<--- Score

205. Is maximizing Security Architectures protection the same as minimizing Security Architectures loss?
<--- Score

206. If you had to rebuild your organization without any traditional competitive advantages (i.e., no killer technology, promising research, innovative product/ service delivery model, etcetera), how would your people have to approach their work and collaborate together in order to create the necessary conditions for success?
<--- Score

Add up total points for this section:
_____ = Total points for this section

Divided by: ______ (number of statements answered) = ______ Average score for this section

Transfer your score to the Security Architectures Index at the beginning of the Self-Assessment.

Security Architectures and Managing Projects, Criteria for Project Managers:

1.0 Initiating Process Group: Security Architectures

1. Were decisions made in a timely manner?

2. Do you understand all business (operational), technical, resource and vendor risks associated with the Security Architectures project?

3. What will be the pressing issues of tomorrow?

4. Were sponsors and decision makers available when needed outside regularly scheduled meetings?

5. What are the tools and techniques to be used in each phase?

6. What were the challenges that you encountered during the execution of a previous Security Architectures project that you would not want to repeat?

7. Contingency planning. if a risk event occurs, what will you do?

8. Who is involved in each phase?

9. Are you properly tracking the progress of the Security Architectures project and communicating the status to stakeholders?

10. What are the pressing issues of the hour?

11. Do you know the roles & responsibilities required for this Security Architectures project?

12. Are you just doing busywork to pass the time?

13. What were things that you need to improve?

14. Do you understand the quality and control criteria that must be achieved for successful Security Architectures project completion?

15. What is the NEXT thing to do?

16. Which of six sigmas dmaic phases focuses on the measurement of internal process that affect factors that are critical to quality?

17. Does it make any difference if you am successful?

18. When are the deliverables to be generated in each phase?

19. What business situation is being addressed?

20. Do you know all the stakeholders impacted by the Security Architectures project and what needs are?

1.1 Project Charter: Security Architectures

21. Run it as as a startup?

22. What are you striving to accomplish (measurable goal(s))?

23. Is it an improvement over existing products?

24. How will you know that a change is an improvement?

25. What barriers do you predict to your success?

26. What changes can you make to improve?

27. Market – identify products market, including whether it is outside of the objective: what is the purpose of the program or Security Architectures project?

28. What goes into your Security Architectures project Charter?

29. Customer benefits: what customer requirements does this Security Architectures project address?

30. What date will the task finish?

31. What is the business need?

32. Who manages integration?

33. Why have you chosen the aim you have set forth?

34. Why is a Security Architectures project Charter used?

35. Avoid costs, improve service, and/ or comply with a mandate?

36. Dependent Security Architectures projects: what Security Architectures projects must be underway or completed before this Security Architectures project can be successful?

37. Why use a Security Architectures project charter?

38. What are some examples of a business case?

39. Name and describe the elements that deal with providing the detail?

1.2 Stakeholder Register: Security Architectures

40. What & Why?

41. What is the power of the stakeholder?

42. Who is managing stakeholder engagement?

43. What are the major Security Architectures project milestones requiring communications or providing communications opportunities?

44. How much influence do they have on the Security Architectures project?

45. Who are the stakeholders?

46. How will reports be created?

47. How should employers make voices heard?

48. How big is the gap?

49. Who wants to talk about Security?

50. What opportunities exist to provide communications?

51. Is your organization ready for change?

1.3 Stakeholder Analysis Matrix: Security Architectures

52. What makes a person a stakeholder?

53. Who influences whom?

54. Which conditions out of the control of the management are crucial for the achievement of the immediate objective?

55. What do people from other organizations see as your organizations weaknesses?

56. What unique or lowest-cost resources does the Security Architectures project have access to?

57. Will the impacts be local, national or international?

58. What could your organization improve?

59. Where are the good opportunities facing your organizations development?

60. What advantages do your organizations stakeholders have?

61. Marketing - reach, distribution, awareness?

62. Which resources are required?

63. Participatory approach: how will key stakeholders participate in the Security Architectures project?

64. Does your organization have bad debt or cash-flow problems?

65. Arena: in what fields are the actors active, where are they present?

66. Disadvantages of proposition?

67. Who has been involved in the area (thematic or geographic) in the past?

68. Global influences?

69. Effects on core activities, distraction?

70. Are there different rules or organizational models for men and women?

71. How can you fill the need to show progress?

2.0 Planning Process Group: Security Architectures

72. Is the Security Architectures project supported by national and/or local organizations?

73. To what extent and in what ways are the Security Architectures project contributing to progress towards organizational reform?

74. In what ways can the governance of the Security Architectures project be improved so that it has greater likelihood of achieving future sustainability?

75. On which process should team members spend the most time?

76. Are work methodologies, financial instruments, etc. shared among departments, organizations and Security Architectures projects?

77. To what extent do the intervention objectives and strategies of the Security Architectures project respond to your organizations plans?

78. Who are the Security Architectures project stakeholders?

79. How well defined and documented are the Security Architectures project management processes you chose to use?

80. You are creating your WBS and find that you keep

decomposing tasks into smaller and smaller units. How can you tell when you are done?

81. Did you read it correctly?

82. If task x starts two days late, what is the effect on the Security Architectures project end date?

83. Does the program have follow-up mechanisms (to verify the quality of the products, punctuality of delivery, etc.) to measure progress in the achievement of the envisaged results?

84. In which Security Architectures project management process group is the detailed Security Architectures project budget created?

85. How are it Security Architectures projects different?

86. What will you do to minimize the impact should a risk event occur?

87. How are the principles of aid effectiveness (ownership, alignment, management for development results and mutual responsibility) being applied in the Security Architectures project?

88. To what extent are the participating departments coordinating with each other?

89. Will you be replaced?

90. To what extent has the intervention strategy been adapted to the areas of intervention in which it is being implemented?

91. Are there efficient coordination mechanisms to avoid overloading the counterparts, participating stakeholders?

2.1 Project Management Plan: Security Architectures

92. What are the deliverables?

93. Why do you manage integration?

94. Is mitigation authorized or recommended?

95. Does the selected plan protect privacy?

96. When is the Security Architectures project management plan created?

97. What happened during the process that you found interesting?

98. What are the known stakeholder requirements?

99. If the Security Architectures project management plan is a comprehensive document that guides you in Security Architectures project execution and control, then what should it NOT contain?

100. How can you best help your organization to develop consistent practices in Security Architectures project management planning stages?

101. How do you manage time?

102. Did the planning effort collaborate to develop solutions that integrate expertise, policies, programs, and Security Architectures projects across entities?

103. Development trends and opportunities. What if the positive direction and vision of your organization causes expected trends to change?

104. What went wrong?

105. Are the existing and future without-plan conditions reasonable and appropriate?

106. What would you do differently what did not work?

107. What data/reports/tools/etc. do your PMs need?

108. Was the peer (technical) review of the cost estimates duly coordinated with the cost estimate center of expertise and addressed in the review documentation and certification?

109. Are alternatives safe, functional, constructible, economical, reasonable and sustainable?

110. Is the budget realistic?

2.2 Scope Management Plan: Security Architectures

111. How do you know how you are doing?

112. Are Security Architectures project contact logs kept up to date?

113. What happens if scope changes?

114. What are the risks of not having good inter-organization cooperation on the Security Architectures project?

115. Is there a set of procedures defining the scope, procedures, and deliverables defining quality control?

116. Materials available for performing the work?

117. Will your organizations estimating methodology be used and followed?

118. Have the procedures for identifying variances from estimates & adjusting the detailed work program been followed?

119. Are all resource assumptions documented?

120. What does the critical path really mean?

121. What is the relative power of the Security Architectures project manager?

122. How do you know when you are finished?

123. Does the Security Architectures project have a Quality Culture?

124. What are the acceptance criteria (process and criteria to be met for key stakeholder acceptance) and who is authorized to sign off?

125. Are funding resource estimates sufficiently detailed and documented for use in planning and tracking the Security Architectures project?

126. Have all involved Security Architectures project stakeholders and work groups committed to the Security Architectures project?

127. Are estimating assumptions and constraints captured?

128. How much money have you spent?

129. Do Security Architectures project managers participating in the Security Architectures project know the Security Architectures projects true status first hand?

2.3 Requirements Management Plan: Security Architectures

130. Who will finally present the work or product(s) for acceptance?

131. Which hardware or software, related to, or as outcome of the Security Architectures project is new to your organization?

132. Why manage requirements?

133. To see if a requirement statement is sufficiently well-defined, read it from the developers perspective. Mentally add the phrase, call me when youre done to the end of the requirement and see if that makes you nervous. In other words, would you need additional clarification from the author to understand the requirement well enough to design and implement it?

134. If it exists, where is it housed?

135. Do you have an appropriate arrangement for meetings?

136. Is infrastructure setup part of your Security Architectures project?

137. What information regarding the Security Architectures project requirements will be reported?

138. Will the product release be stable and mature enough to be deployed in the user community?

139. The wbs is developed as part of a joint planning session. and how do you know that youhave done this right?

140. Who is responsible for monitoring and tracking the Security Architectures project requirements?

141. Is the system software (non-operating system) new to the IT Security Architectures project team?

142. Define the help desk model. who will take full responsibility?

143. Will you perform a Requirements Risk assessment and develop a plan to deal with risks?

144. What are you trying to do?

145. Do you really need to write this document at all?

146. Business analysis scope?

147. Are actual resources expenditures versus planned expenditures acceptable?

148. How knowledgeable is the primary Stakeholder(s) in the proposed application area?

149. How will bidders price evaluations be done, by deliverables, phases, or in a big bang?

2.4 Requirements Documentation: Security Architectures

150. How do you know when a Requirement is accurate enough?

151. Are all functions required by the customer included?

152. What are the acceptance criteria?

153. How will requirements be documented and who signs off on them?

154. Validity. does the system provide the functions which best support the customers needs?

155. What variations exist for a process?

156. What are the potential disadvantages/ advantages?

157. Where do you define what is a customer, what are the attributes of customer?

158. Where do system and software requirements come from, what are sources?

159. Basic work/business process; high-level, what is being touched?

160. How much does requirements engineering cost?

161. Who provides requirements?

162. How do you get the user to tell you what they want?

163. How linear / iterative is your Requirements Gathering process (or will it be)?

164. What is the risk associated with the technology?

165. Have the benefits identified with the system being identified clearly?

166. Does your organization restrict technical alternatives?

167. Completeness. are all functions required by the customer included?

168. Verifiability. can the requirements be checked?

169. Do technical resources exist?

2.5 Requirements Traceability Matrix: Security Architectures

170. Is there a requirements traceability process in place?

171. How do you manage scope?

172. Why use a WBS?

173. What are the chronologies, contingencies, consequences, criteria?

174. Why do you manage scope?

175. Describe the process for approving requirements so they can be added to the traceability matrix and Security Architectures project work can be performed. Will the Security Architectures project requirements become approved in writing?

176. What percentage of Security Architectures projects are producing traceability matrices between requirements and other work products?

177. How will it affect the stakeholders personally in career?

178. Do you have a clear understanding of all subcontracts in place?

179. Will you use a Requirements Traceability Matrix?

180. What is the WBS?

181. How small is small enough?

2.6 Project Scope Statement: Security Architectures

182. Do you anticipate new stakeholders joining the Security Architectures project over time?

183. Will the risk plan be updated on a regular and frequent basis?

184. Is the quality function identified and assigned?

185. Elements that deal with providing the detail?

186. Was planning completed before the Security Architectures project was initiated?

187. What should you drop in order to add something new?

188. If the scope changes, what will the impact be to your Security Architectures project in terms of duration, cost, quality, or any other important areas of the Security Architectures project?

189. How often will scope changes be reviewed?

190. Will an issue form be in use?

191. Is this process communicated to the customer and team members?

192. If there is an independent oversight contractor, have they signed off on the Security Architectures

project Plan?

193. Is there a Change Management Board?

194. What is change?

195. Why do you need to manage scope?

196. Are there issues that could affect the existing requirements for the result, service, or product if the scope changes?

197. What went right?

198. Will all Security Architectures project issues be unconditionally tracked through the issue resolution process?

199. Is the plan for your organization of the Security Architectures project resources adequate?

200. Were potential customers involved early in the planning process?

2.7 Assumption and Constraint Log: Security Architectures

201. Has a Security Architectures project Communications Plan been developed?

202. What if failure during recovery?

203. Is the process working, and people are not executing in compliance of the process?

204. What is positive about the current process?

205. Are best practices and metrics employed to identify issues, progress, performance, etc.?

206. Have you eliminated all duplicative tasks or manual efforts, where appropriate?

207. Diagrams and tables are included to account for complex concepts and increase overall readability?

208. What does an audit system look like?

209. Violation trace: why ?

210. Is this model reasonable?

211. If appropriate, is the deliverable content consistent with current Security Architectures project documents and in compliance with the Document Management Plan?

212. Does a specific action and/or state that is known to violate security policy occur?

213. Security analysis has access to information that is sanitized?

214. Is the amount of effort justified by the anticipated value of forming a new process?

215. Model-building: what data-analytic strategies are useful when building proportional-hazards models?

216. What do you audit?

217. Does the traceability documentation describe the tool and/or mechanism to be used to capture traceability throughout the life cycle?

218. Have adequate resources been provided by management to ensure Security Architectures project success?

219. Is the current scope of the Security Architectures project substantially different than that originally defined in the approved Security Architectures project plan?

220. Do documented requirements exist for all critical components and areas, including technical, business, interfaces, performance, security and conversion requirements?

2.8 Work Breakdown Structure: Security Architectures

221. How many levels?

222. Who has to do it?

223. How much detail?

224. How will you and your Security Architectures project team define the Security Architectures projects scope and work breakdown structure?

225. When would you develop a Work Breakdown Structure?

226. What is the probability of completing the Security Architectures project in less that xx days?

227. How big is a work-package?

228. Can you make it?

229. What is the probability that the Security Architectures project duration will exceed xx weeks?

230. When does it have to be done?

231. Where does it take place?

232. Is the work breakdown structure (wbs) defined and is the scope of the Security Architectures project clear with assigned deliverable owners?

233. How far down?

234. When do you stop?

235. Why is it useful?

236. Is it a change in scope?

2.9 WBS Dictionary: Security Architectures

237. Does the accounting system provide a basis for auditing records of direct costs chargeable to the contract?

238. Are control accounts opened and closed based on the start and completion of work contained therein?

239. Are the responsibilities and authorities of each of the above organizational elements or managers clearly defined?

240. Are retroactive changes to direct costs and indirect costs prohibited except for the correction of errors and routine accounting adjustments?

241. Are indirect costs accumulated for comparison with the corresponding budgets?

242. Are the overhead pools formally and adequately identified?

243. Is cost and schedule performance measurement done in a consistent, systematic manner?

244. Is each control account assigned to a single organizational element directly responsible for the work and identifiable to a single element of the CWBS?

245. Is all budget available as management reserve identified and excluded from the performance measurement baseline?

246. Are the bases and rates for allocating costs from each indirect pool to commercial work consistent with the already stated used to allocate corresponding costs to Government contracts?

247. Budgets assigned to major functional organizations?

248. Do work packages reflect the actual way in which the work will be done and are they meaningful products or management-oriented subdivisions of a higher level element of work?

249. Identify potential or actual overruns and underruns?

250. Does the scheduling system provide for the identification of work progress against technical and other milestones, and also provide for forecasts of completion dates of scheduled work?

251. Are the variances between budgeted and actual indirect costs identified and analyzed at the level of assigned responsibility for control (indirect pool, department, etc.)?

252. Are estimates developed by Security Architectures project personnel coordinated with the already stated responsible for overall management to determine whether required resources will be available according to revised planning?

253. Does the contractor use objective results, design reviews and tests to trace schedule performance?

254. Is work properly classified as measured effort, LOE, or apportioned effort and appropriately separated?

2.10 Schedule Management Plan: Security Architectures

255. Is the schedule feasible and at what cost?

256. Has a structured approach been used to break work effort into manageable components (WBS)?

257. What will be the final cost of the Security Architectures project if status quo is maintained?

258. Pareto diagrams, statistical sampling, flow charting or trend analysis used quality monitoring?

259. Has a provision been made to reassess Security Architectures project risks at various Security Architectures project stages?

260. Will rolling way planning be used?

261. Were the budget estimates reasonable?

262. Are issues raised, assessed, actioned, and resolved in a timely and efficient manner?

263. Is the communication plan being followed?

264. Are internal Security Architectures project status meetings held at reasonable intervals?

265. Does the Security Architectures project have a Quality Culture?

266. Have stakeholder accountabilities & responsibilities been clearly defined?

267. Do Security Architectures project managers participating in the Security Architectures project know the Security Architectures projects true status first hand?

268. Are changes in scope (deliverable commitments) agreed to by all affected groups & individuals?

269. Is there general agreement & acceptance of the current status and progress of the Security Architectures project?

270. Is there an issues management plan in place?

271. Is there any form of automated support for Issues Management?

272. Are all activities captured and do they address all approved work scope in the Security Architectures project baseline?

273. Has the budget been baselined?

2.11 Activity List: Security Architectures

274. Is infrastructure setup part of your Security Architectures project?

275. For other activities, how much delay can be tolerated?

276. How should ongoing costs be monitored to try to keep the Security Architectures project within budget?

277. Where will it be performed?

278. In what sequence?

279. What are the critical bottleneck activities?

280. When will the work be performed?

281. What did not go as well?

282. Should you include sub-activities?

283. What is the LF and LS for each activity?

284. How detailed should a Security Architectures project get?

285. How difficult will it be to do specific activities on this Security Architectures project?

286. How will it be performed?

287. Can you determine the activity that must finish, before this activity can start?

288. What is the total time required to complete the Security Architectures project if no delays occur?

289. How much slack is available in the Security Architectures project?

290. How do you determine the late start (LS) for each activity?

291. What went well?

2.12 Activity Attributes: Security Architectures

292. Why?

293. What conclusions/generalizations can you draw from this?

294. Have you identified the Activity Leveling Priority code value on each activity?

295. What is missing?

296. How many resources do you need to complete the work scope within a limit of X number of days?

297. How many days do you need to complete the work scope with a limit of X number of resources?

298. Have constraints been applied to the start and finish milestones for the phases?

299. Can more resources be added?

300. Are the required resources available or need to be acquired?

301. What is your organizations history in doing similar activities?

302. Which method produces the more accurate cost assignment?

303. How else could the items be grouped?

304. Where else does it apply?

305. How difficult will it be to do specific activities on this Security Architectures project?

306. What activity do you think you should spend the most time on?

307. Do you feel very comfortable with your prediction?

308. How difficult will it be to complete specific activities on this Security Architectures project?

309. Resources to accomplish the work?

310. Is there a trend during the year?

2.13 Milestone List: Security Architectures

311. What are your competitors vulnerabilities?

312. How will you get the word out to customers?

313. What has been done so far?

314. What is the market for your technology, product or service?

315. Sustaining internal capabilities?

316. What background experience, skills, and strengths does the team bring to your organization?

317. How difficult will it be to do specific activities on this Security Architectures project?

318. When will the Security Architectures project be complete?

319. How soon can the activity finish?

320. Which path is the critical path?

321. Sustainable financial backing?

322. Gaps in capabilities?

323. Who will manage the Security Architectures project on a day-to-day basis?

324. Competitive advantages?

325. Level of the Innovation?

326. Obstacles faced?

327. Calculate how long can activity be delayed?

328. Loss of key staff?

2.14 Network Diagram: Security Architectures

329. Can you calculate the confidence level?

330. How confident can you be in your milestone dates and the delivery date?

331. What must be completed before an activity can be started?

332. If x is long, what would be the completion time if you break x into two parallel parts of y weeks and z weeks?

333. What controls the start and finish of a job?

334. What is the completion time?

335. If the Security Architectures project network diagram cannot change and you have extra personnel resources, what is the BEST thing to do?

336. What are the Key Success Factors?

337. Where do schedules come from?

338. What are the tools?

339. Which type of network diagram allows you to depict four types of dependencies?

340. What to do and When?

341. What is the probability of completing the Security Architectures project in less that xx days?

342. What job or jobs precede it?

343. What job or jobs could run concurrently?

344. Will crashing x weeks return more in benefits than it costs?

345. Are the gantt chart and/or network diagram updated periodically and used to assess the overall Security Architectures project timetable?

346. What activities must occur simultaneously with this activity?

347. How difficult will it be to do specific activities on this Security Architectures project?

2.15 Activity Resource Requirements: Security Architectures

348. Why do you do that?

349. Which logical relationship does the PDM use most often?

350. Other support in specific areas?

351. Are there unresolved issues that need to be addressed?

352. Organizational Applicability?

353. What are constraints that you might find during the Human Resource Planning process?

354. Anything else?

355. Is there anything planned that does not need to be here?

356. How many signatures do you require on a check and does this match what is in your policy and procedures?

357. How do you handle petty cash?

358. When does monitoring begin?

359. Do you use tools like decomposition and rolling-wave planning to produce the activity list and other

outputs?

360. Time for overtime?

361. What is the Work Plan Standard?

2.16 Resource Breakdown Structure: Security Architectures

362. What is the primary purpose of the human resource plan?

363. Any changes from stakeholders?

364. What is the difference between % Complete and % work?

365. Why is this important?

366. Which resource planning tool provides information on resource responsibility and accountability?

367. Who needs what information?

368. Is predictive resource analysis being done?

369. What defines a successful Security Architectures project?

370. Who is allowed to see what data about which resources?

371. Who is allowed to perform which functions?

372. Why do you do it?

373. What is the purpose of assigning and documenting responsibility?

374. What is Security Architectures project communication management?

375. Who delivers the information?

376. What is each stakeholders desired outcome for the Security Architectures project?

377. Who will use the system?

2.17 Activity Duration Estimates: Security Architectures

378. What are the main processes included in Security Architectures project quality management?

379. Is corrective action taken to bring Security Architectures project performance into line with the Security Architectures project plan?

380. What are the main types of contracts if you do decide to outsource?

381. How many different communications channels does a Security Architectures project team with six people have?

382. Are procedures followed to ensure information is available to stakeholders in a timely manner?

383. Consider the changes in the job market for information technology workers. How does the job market and current state of the economy affect human resource management?

384. Why is it important to determine activity sequencing on Security Architectures projects?

385. If you plan to take the PMP exam soon, what should you do to prepare?

386. When would a milestone chart be used instead of a bar char?

387. List five reasons why organizations outsource. Why is there a growing trend in outsourcing, especially in the government?

388. Who will provide inputs for it?

389. Have most organizations benefited from outsourcing?

390. How does the job market and current state of the economy affect human resource management?

391. How can others help Security Architectures project managers understand your organizational context for Security Architectures projects?

392. Calculate the expected duration for an activity that has a most likely time of 3, a pessimistic time of 10, and a optimiztic time of 2?

393. Do procedures exist describing how the Security Architectures project scope will be managed?

394. What steps did your organization take to earn this prestigious quality award?

395. Explanation notice how many choices are half right?

396. Are risks that are likely to affect the Security Architectures project identified and documented?

397. Do they make sense?

2.18 Duration Estimating Worksheet: Security Architectures

398. Small or large Security Architectures project?

399. Will the Security Architectures project collaborate with the local community and leverage resources?

400. What info is needed?

401. Do any colleagues have experience with your organization and/or RFPs?

402. Does the Security Architectures project provide innovative ways for stakeholders to overcome obstacles or deliver better outcomes?

403. When do the individual activities need to start and finish?

404. Why estimate time and cost?

405. Can the Security Architectures project be constructed as planned?

406. What is an Average Security Architectures project?

407. What is the total time required to complete the Security Architectures project if no delays occur?

408. What is next?

409. How should ongoing costs be monitored to try to keep the Security Architectures project within budget?

410. Is the Security Architectures project responsive to community need?

411. Value pocket identification & quantification what are value pockets?

412. What questions do you have?

413. What utility impacts are there?

2.19 Project Schedule: Security Architectures

414. Why do you need schedules?

415. Is Security Architectures project work proceeding in accordance with the original Security Architectures project schedule?

416. To what degree is do you feel the entire team was committed to the Security Architectures project schedule?

417. Month Security Architectures project take?

418. Eliminate unnecessary activities. Are there activities that came from a template or previous Security Architectures project that are not applicable on this phase of this Security Architectures project?

419. Did the final product meet or exceed user expectations?

420. What is the purpose of a Security Architectures project schedule?

421. How do you manage Security Architectures project Risk?

422. Verify that the update is accurate. Are all remaining durations correct?

423. Are the original Security Architectures project

schedule and budget realistic?

424. What is Security Architectures project management?

425. Your Security Architectures project management plan results in a Security Architectures project schedule that is too long. If the Security Architectures project network diagram cannot change and you have extra personnel resources, what is the BEST thing to do?

426. Are there activities that came from a template or previous Security Architectures project that are not applicable on this phase of this Security Architectures project?

427. How effectively were issues able to be resolved without impacting the Security Architectures project Schedule or Budget?

428. Are procedures defined by which the Security Architectures project schedule may be changed?

429. It allows the Security Architectures project to be delivered on schedule. How Do you Use Schedules?

430. Schedule/cost recovery?

431. Why do you need to manage Security Architectures project Risk?

432. Did the Security Architectures project come in on schedule?

433. Master Security Architectures project schedule?

2.20 Cost Management Plan: Security Architectures

434. Timeline and milestones?

435. Has a sponsor been identified?

436. Cost management – how will the cost of changes be estimated and controlled?

437. Is the schedule updated on a periodic basis?

438. What is your organizations history in doing similar tasks?

439. Are the quality tools and methods identified in the Quality Plan appropriate to the Security Architectures project?

440. Was the scope definition used in task sequencing?

441. Are the Security Architectures project plans updated on a frequent basis?

442. Vac -variance at completion, how much over/ under budget do you expect to be?

443. Are the payment terms being followed?

444. Have reserves been created to address risks?

445. Is there anything unique in this Security

Architectures projects scope statement that will affect resources?

446. Have adequate resources been provided by management to ensure Security Architectures project success?

447. Does the detailed work plan match the complexity of tasks with the capabilities of personnel?

448. Do Security Architectures project teams & team members report on status / activities / progress?

449. Scope of work – What is the scope of work for each of the planned contracts?

450. Have all documents been archived in a Security Architectures project repository for each release?

451. What weaknesses do you have?

2.21 Activity Cost Estimates: Security Architectures

452. When do you enter into PPM?

453. Were escalated issues resolved promptly?

454. Are data needed on characteristics of care?

455. How do you fund change orders?

456. What is the activity recast of the budget?

457. What is the activity inventory?

458. What communication items need improvement?

459. What were things that you did well, and could improve, and how?

460. Were the costs or charges reasonable?

461. What areas does the group agree are the biggest success on the Security Architectures project?

462. Who determines when the contractor is paid?

463. Were the tasks or work products prepared by the consultant useful?

464. Can you delete activities or make them inactive?

465. How and when do you enter into Security

Architectures project Procurement Management?

466. How do you change activities?

467. What is the last item a Security Architectures project manager must do to finalize Security Architectures project close-out?

468. How Award?

469. Who & what determines the need for contracted services?

470. Can you change your activities?

471. What were things that you did very well and want to do the same again on the next Security Architectures project?

2.22 Cost Estimating Worksheet: Security Architectures

472. Does the Security Architectures project provide innovative ways for stakeholders to overcome obstacles or deliver better outcomes?

473. What is the purpose of estimating?

474. Is the Security Architectures project responsive to community need?

475. Ask: are others positioned to know, are others credible, and will others cooperate?

476. What can be included?

477. Is it feasible to establish a control group arrangement?

478. Will the Security Architectures project collaborate with the local community and leverage resources?

479. What additional Security Architectures project(s) could be initiated as a result of this Security Architectures project?

480. What happens to any remaining funds not used?

481. Who is best positioned to know and assist in identifying corresponding factors?

482. What costs are to be estimated?

483. Identify the timeframe necessary to monitor progress and collect data to determine how the selected measure has changed?

484. What will others want?

485. What is the estimated labor cost today based upon this information?

486. How will the results be shared and to whom?

487. Can a trend be established from historical performance data on the selected measure and are the criteria for using trend analysis or forecasting methods met?

2.23 Cost Baseline: Security Architectures

488. Verify business objectives. Are others appropriate, and well-articulated?

489. Has the actual cost of the Security Architectures project (or Security Architectures project phase) been tallied and compared to the approved budget?

490. Have the lessons learned been filed with the Security Architectures project Management Office?

491. How likely is it to go wrong?

492. At which frequency ?

493. Where do changes come from?

494. How difficult will it be to do specific tasks on the Security Architectures project?

495. How will cost estimates be used?

496. On budget?

497. Has the appropriate access to relevant data and analysis capability been granted?

498. Does it impact schedule, cost, quality?

499. Have all approved changes to the cost baseline been identified and impact on the Security

Architectures project documented?

500. What is the most important thing to do next to make your Security Architectures project successful?

501. Is there anything you need from upper management in order to be successful?

502. Has training and knowledge transfer of the operations organization been completed?

503. Has the Security Architectures projected annual cost to operate and maintain the product(s) or service(s) been approved and funded?

504. Definition of done can be traced back to the definitions of what are you providing to the customer in terms of deliverables?

2.24 Quality Management Plan: Security Architectures

505. What are your organizations key processes (product, service, business, and support)?

506. What key performance indicators does your organization use to measure, manage, and improve key processes?

507. Have all necessary approvals been obtained?

508. How do you ensure that protocols are up to date?

509. What would be the next steps or what else should you do at this point?

510. After observing execution of process, is it in compliance with the documented Plan?

511. Documented results available?

512. Can you perform this task or activity in a more effective manner?

513. What is your organizations strategic planning process?

514. Sampling part of task?

515. Who is responsible for writing the qapp?

516. Are requirements management tracking tools

and procedures in place?

517. With the five whys method, the team considers why the issue being explored occurred. do others then take that initial answer and ask why?

518. How do you ensure that your sampling methods and procedures meet your data quality objectives?

519. What are your organizations current levels and trends for the already stated measures related to customer satisfaction/ dissatisfaction and product/ service performance?

520. Does the program use other agents to collect samples?

521. Are there processes in place to ensure internal consistency between the source code components?

522. Are you meeting the quality standards?

523. Who gets results of work?

2.25 Quality Metrics: Security Architectures

524. Are there already quality metrics available that detect nonlinear embeddings and trends similar to the users perception?

525. What are your organizations expectations for its quality Security Architectures project?

526. How do you calculate such metrics?

527. Were number of defects identified?

528. Filter visualizations of interest?

529. What method of measurement do you use?

530. What is the CMS Benchmark?

531. Is the reporting frequency appropriate?

532. What documentation is required?

533. What are you trying to accomplish?

534. How do you calculate corresponding metrics?

535. Are documents on hand to provide explanations of privacy and confidentiality?

536. Should a modifier be included?

537. Can visual measures help you to filter visualizations of interest?

538. When is the security analysis testing complete?

539. Does risk analysis documentation meet standards?

540. Are there any open risk issues?

541. Who notifies stakeholders of normal and abnormal results?

542. Is quality culture a competitive advantage?

543. Which report did you use to create the data you are submitting?

2.26 Process Improvement Plan: Security Architectures

544. What personnel are the champions for the initiative?

545. Have the supporting tools been developed or acquired?

546. Where do you want to be?

547. Why quality management?

548. To elicit goal statements, do you ask a question such as, What do you want to achieve?

549. What is quality and how will you ensure it?

550. Where are you now?

551. Everyone agrees on what process improvement is, right?

552. Management commitment at all levels?

553. What makes people good SPI coaches?

554. Who should prepare the process improvement action plan?

555. How do you manage quality?

556. What personnel are the sponsors for that

initiative?

557. How do you measure?

558. What personnel are the coaches for your initiative?

559. Does explicit definition of the measures exist?

560. Modeling current processes is great, and will you ever see a return on that investment?

561. Are you following the quality standards?

562. Have the frequency of collection and the points in the process where measurements will be made been determined?

2.27 Responsibility Assignment Matrix: Security Architectures

563. What will the work cost?

564. Who is going to do that work?

565. The anticipated business volume?

566. What travel needed?

567. If a role has only Signing-off, or only Communicating responsibility and has no Performing, Accountable, or Monitoring responsibility, is it necessary?

568. Do you know how your people are allocated?

569. Are meaningful indicators identified for use in measuring the status of cost and schedule performance?

570. What do people write/say on status/Security Architectures project reports?

571. Are people encouraged to bring up issues?

572. Undistributed budgets, if any?

573. What is the justification?

574. How many people do you need?

575. Are data elements reconcilable between internal summary reports and reports forwarded to stakeholders?

576. Who is responsible for work and budgets for each wbs?

577. Are overhead cost budgets established for each organization which has authority to incur overhead costs?

578. Does the contractors system provide unit or lot costs when applicable?

579. Are estimates of costs at completion generated in a rational, consistent manner?

2.28 Roles and Responsibilities: Security Architectures

580. Authority: what areas/Security Architectures projects in your work do you have the authority to decide upon and act on the already stated decisions?

581. Key conclusions and recommendations: Are conclusions and recommendations relevant and acceptable?

582. Does the team have access to and ability to use data analysis tools?

583. What should you do now to prepare yourself for a promotion, increased responsibilities or a different job?

584. Attainable / achievable: the goal is attainable; can you actually accomplish the goal?

585. To decide whether to use a quality measurement, ask how will you know when it is achieved?

586. Implementation of actions: Who are the responsible units?

587. Are governance roles and responsibilities documented?

588. What specific behaviors did you observe?

589. What expectations were met?

590. How well did the Security Architectures project Team understand the expectations of specific roles and responsibilities?

591. Are Security Architectures project team roles and responsibilities identified and documented?

592. Do you take the time to clearly define roles and responsibilities on Security Architectures project tasks?

593. Do the values and practices inherent in the culture of your organization foster or hinder the process?

594. Influence: what areas of organizational decision making are you able to influence when you do not have authority to make the final decision?

595. What is working well within your organizations performance management system?

596. Is the data complete?

597. Required skills, knowledge, experience?

598. Be specific; avoid generalities. Thank you and great work alone are insufficient. What exactly do you appreciate and why?

599. Are your budgets supportive of a culture of quality data?

2.29 Human Resource Management Plan: Security Architectures

600. Are assumptions being identified, recorded, analyzed, qualified and closed?

601. What areas were overlooked on this Security Architectures project?

602. Is Security Architectures project work proceeding in accordance with the original Security Architectures project schedule?

603. Are quality inspections and review activities listed in the Security Architectures project schedule(s)?

604. Have all documents been archived in a Security Architectures project repository for each release?

605. Is a payment system in place with proper reviews and approvals?

606. How do you determine what key skills and talents are needed to meet the objectives. Is your organization primarily focused on a specific industry?

607. Have external dependencies been captured in the schedule?

608. Is the quality assurance team identified?

609. Are changes in deliverable commitments agreed

to by all affected groups & individuals?

610. Have all unresolved risks been documented?

611. Has the Security Architectures project manager been identified?

612. Have all involved Security Architectures project stakeholders and work groups committed to the Security Architectures project?

613. Does the Security Architectures project have a Statement of Work?

614. Is documentation created for communication with the suppliers and Vendors?

2.30 Communications Management Plan: Security Architectures

615. Where do team members get information?

616. Do you have members of your team responsible for certain stakeholders?

617. Who is the stakeholder?

618. Who to share with?

619. What is the stakeholders level of authority?

620. In your work, how much time is spent on stakeholder identification?

621. Conflict resolution -which method when?

622. What to learn?

623. How much time does it take to do it?

624. Are there too many who have an interest in some aspect of your work?

625. Are others part of the communications management plan?

626. Do you feel a register helps?

627. Who to learn from?

628. Are others needed?

629. What to know?

630. Why manage stakeholders?

631. Do you then often overlook a key stakeholder or stakeholder group?

632. How do you manage communications?

633. Can you think of other people who might have concerns or interests?

634. How is this initiative related to other portfolios, programs, or Security Architectures projects?

2.31 Risk Management Plan: Security Architectures

635. Prioritized components/features?

636. Premium on reliability of product?

637. Could others have been better mitigated?

638. Is the number of people on the Security Architectures project team adequate to do the job?

639. Is the process being followed?

640. Management -what contingency plans do you have if the risk becomes a reality?

641. What other risks are created by choosing an avoidance strategy?

642. How is risk monitoring performed?

643. Are end-users enthusiastically committed to the Security Architectures project and the system/ product to be built?

644. Do requirements put excessive performance constraints on the product?

645. Are there alternative opinions/solutions/ processes you should explore?

646. Are the reports useful and easy to read?

647. Maximize short-term return on investment?

648. Are the best people available?

649. Technology risk: is the Security Architectures project technically feasible?

650. What risks are necessary to achieve success?

651. Do requirements demand the use of new analysis, design, or testing methods?

652. Are some people working on multiple Security Architectures projects?

653. Are requirements fully understood by the software engineering team and customers?

654. If you can not fix it, how do you do it differently?

2.32 Risk Register: Security Architectures

655. Preventative actions - planned actions to reduce the likelihood a risk will occur and/or reduce the seriousness should it occur. What should you do now?

656. How well are risks controlled?

657. How is a Community Risk Register created?

658. What risks might negatively or positively affect achieving the Security Architectures project objectives?

659. What action, if any, has been taken to respond to the risk?

660. Who is accountable?

661. Do you require further engagement?

662. What has changed since the last period?

663. Can the likelihood and impact of failing to achieve corresponding recommendations and action plans be assessed?

664. Recovery actions - planned actions taken once a risk has occurred to allow you to move on. What should you do after?

665. What are your key risks/show istoppers and what

is being done to manage them?

666. How often will the Risk Management Plan and Risk Register be formally reviewed, and by whom?

667. What evidence do you have to justify the likelihood score of the risk (audit, incident report, claim, complaints, inspection, internal review)?

668. What are the major risks facing the Security Architectures project?

669. Have other controls and solutions been implemented in other services which could be applied as an alternative to additional funding?

670. Severity Prediction?

671. Are implemented controls working as others should?

672. Are there any knock-on effects/impact on any of the other areas?

673. How could corresponding Risk affect the Security Architectures project in terms of cost and schedule?

2.33 Probability and Impact Assessment: Security Architectures

674. How would you suggest monitoring for risk transition indicators?

675. Who should be notified of the occurrence of each of the risk indicators?

676. What is the risk appetite?

677. What should be the gestation period for the Security Architectures project with specific technology?

678. Do the requirements require the creation of new algorithms?

679. What is the impact if the risk does occur?

680. How much is the probability of a risk occurring?

681. What things are likely to change?

682. What can you do about it?

683. Which functions, departments, and activities of your organization are going to be affected?

684. Which of your Security Architectures projects should be selected when compared with other Security Architectures projects?

685. What will be the likely political environment during the life of the Security Architectures project?

686. Are the risk data timely and relevant?

687. Who are the international/overseas Security Architectures project partners (equipment supplier/supplier/consultant/contractor) for this Security Architectures project?

688. Can the risk be avoided by choosing a different alternative?

689. What things might go wrong?

690. Are the facilities, expertise, resources, and management know-how available to handle the situation?

691. Which of corresponding risk factors can be avoided altogether?

692. Is the present organizational structure for handling the Security Architectures project sufficient?

2.34 Probability and Impact Matrix: Security Architectures

693. Can you handle the investment risk?

694. Are people attending meetings and doing work?

695. Are Security Architectures project requirements stable?

696. Degree of confidence in estimated size estimate?

697. What are the levels of understanding of the future users of this technology?

698. How much is the probability of the risk occurring?

699. How should you structure risks?

700. What needs to be DONE?

701. Have staff received necessary training?

702. What risks were tracked?

703. Economic to take on the Security Architectures project?

704. What are the methods to deal with risks?

705. During which risk management process is a determination to transfer a risk made?

706. How do you analyze the risks in the different types of Security Architectures projects?

707. Workarounds are determined during which risk management process?

708. What is the best method for analysing the risks for different types of Security Architectures projects?

709. What would you do differently?

710. Which role do you have in the Security Architectures project?

711. Are the risk data complete?

2.35 Risk Data Sheet: Security Architectures

712. Whom do you serve (customers)?

713. What can you do?

714. Are new hazards created?

715. Has a sensitivity analysis been carried out?

716. Has the most cost-effective solution been chosen?

717. What if client refuses?

718. What are you here for (Mission)?

719. How can it happen?

720. Potential for recurrence?

721. What can happen?

722. What actions can be taken to eliminate or remove risk?

723. What do people affected think about the need for, and practicality of preventive measures?

724. What will be the consequences if it happens?

725. What are you trying to achieve (Objectives)?

726. What is the environment within which you operate (social trends, economic, community values, broad based participation, national directions etc.)?

727. If it happens, what are the consequences?

2.36 Procurement Management Plan: Security Architectures

728. What types of contracts will be used?

729. Are any non-compliance issues that exist communicated to your organization?

730. Is there an approved case?

731. Is pert / critical path or equivalent methodology being used?

732. Are Security Architectures project team members involved in detailed estimating and scheduling?

733. Are status reports received per the Security Architectures project Plan?

734. Measurable - are the targets measurable?

735. Was an original risk assessment/risk management plan completed?

736. Is the Security Architectures project sponsor clearly communicating the business case or rationale for why this Security Architectures project is needed?

737. Has a Security Architectures project Communications Plan been developed?

738. Has a provision been made to reassess Security Architectures project risks at various Security

Architectures project stages?

739. Is it standard practice to formally commit stakeholders to the Security Architectures project via agreements?

740. Are metrics used to evaluate and manage Vendors?

741. Does the business case include how the Security Architectures project aligns with your organizations strategic goals & objectives?

742. Have Security Architectures project management standards and procedures been identified / established and documented?

743. Are the Security Architectures project team members located locally to the users/stakeholders?

744. Has a quality assurance plan been developed for the Security Architectures project?

2.37 Source Selection Criteria: Security Architectures

745. How should oral presentations be evaluated?

746. How do you encourage efficiency and consistency?

747. What is the role of counsel in the procurement process?

748. When must you conduct a debriefing?

749. Can you make a cost/technical tradeoff?

750. What are the special considerations for preaward debriefings?

751. Does your documentation identify why the team concurs or differs with reported performance from past performance report (CPARs, questionnaire responses, etc.)?

752. What should a DRFP include?

753. What evidence should be provided regarding proposal evaluations?

754. When and what information can be considered with offerors regarding past performance?

755. How should the oral presentations be handled?

756. What management structure does your organization consider as optimal for performing the contract?

757. Do you want to have them collaborate at subfactor level?

758. What are the guiding principles for developing an evaluation report?

759. Are there any specific considerations that precludes offers from being selected as the awardee?

760. In which phase of the acquisition process cycle does source qualifications reside?

761. What are the most critical evaluation criteria that prove to be tiebreakers in the evaluation of proposals?

762. In order of importance, which evaluation criteria are the most critical to the determination of your overall rating?

763. Do you prepare an independent cost estimate?

764. How will you decide an evaluators write up is sufficient?

2.38 Stakeholder Management Plan: Security Architectures

765. Were Security Architectures project team members involved in detailed estimating and scheduling?

766. Where to get additional help?

767. Alignment to strategic goals & objectives?

768. Does this include subcontracted development?

769. Does all Security Architectures project documentation reside in a common repository for easy access?

770. Are Security Architectures project leaders committed to this Security Architectures project full time?

771. What potential impact does the Security Architectures project have on the stakeholder?

772. Are Security Architectures project team members committed fulltime?

773. Are there unnecessary steps that are creating bottlenecks and/or causing people to wait?

774. Are decisions captured in a decisions log?

775. Are the appropriate IT resources adequate to

meet planned commitments?

776. Is there an onboarding process in place?

777. What other teams / processes would be impacted by changes to the current process, and how?

778. Is there a formal set of procedures supporting Stakeholder Management?

779. Are tasks tracked by hours?

780. Does the Security Architectures project have a Statement of Work?

781. Has the scope management document been updated and distributed to help prevent scope creep?

2.39 Change Management Plan: Security Architectures

782. What will be the preferred method of delivery?

783. What would be an estimate of the total cost for the activities required to carry out the change initiative?

784. What policies and procedures need to be changed?

785. Do you need a new organizational structure?

786. Is it the same for each of the business units?

787. Are work location changes required?

788. What are the specific target groups / audience that will be impacted by this change?

789. What are the training strategies?

790. Has the target training audience been identified and nominated?

791. Change invariability confront many relationships especially the already stated that require a set of behaviours What roles with in your organization are affected and how?

792. Why would a Security Architectures project run more smoothly when change management is

emphasized from the beginning?

793. What method and medium would you use to announce a message?

794. What are the major changes to processes?

795. Has the training provider been established?

796. What communication network would you use – informal or formal?

797. Who might be able to help you the most?

798. What do you expect the target audience to do, say, think or feel as a result of this communication?

799. Who is the audience for change management activities?

800. What work practices will be affected?

3.0 Executing Process Group: Security Architectures

801. What are the main processes included in Security Architectures project quality management?

802. How well did the team follow the chosen processes?

803. What good practices or successful experiences or transferable examples have been identified?

804. Just how important is your work to the overall success of the Security Architectures project?

805. If action is called for, what form should it take?

806. Are decisions made in a timely manner?

807. What areas were overlooked on this Security Architectures project?

808. How can software assist in procuring goods and services?

809. What type of information goes in the quality assurance plan?

810. What are crucial elements of successful Security Architectures project plan execution?

811. What are deliverables of your Security Architectures project?

812. Will new hardware or software be required for servers or client machines?

813. Do the partners have sufficient financial capacity to keep up the benefits produced by the programme?

814. Does software appear easy to learn?

815. In what way has the program come up with innovative measures for problem-solving?

816. Is the Security Architectures project performing better or worse than planned?

817. Could a new application negatively affect the current IT infrastructure?

818. What were things that you did very well and want to do the same again on the next Security Architectures project?

3.1 Team Member Status Report: Security Architectures

819. Does your organization have the means (staff, money, contract, etc.) to produce or to acquire the product, good, or service?

820. Will the staff do training or is that done by a third party?

821. Why is it to be done?

822. What is to be done?

823. Are the products of your organizations Security Architectures projects meeting customers objectives?

824. How does this product, good, or service meet the needs of the Security Architectures project and your organization as a whole?

825. Does the product, good, or service already exist within your organization?

826. Do you have an Enterprise Security Architectures project Management Office (EPMO)?

827. Are the attitudes of staff regarding Security Architectures project work improving?

828. Is there evidence that staff is taking a more professional approach toward management of your organizations Security Architectures projects?

829. Are your organizations Security Architectures projects more successful over time?

830. The problem with Reward & Recognition Programs is that the truly deserving people all too often get left out. How can you make it practical?

831. How much risk is involved?

832. What specific interest groups do you have in place?

833. When a teams productivity and success depend on collaboration and the efficient flow of information, what generally fails them?

834. How can you make it practical?

835. How it is to be done?

836. Does every department have to have a Security Architectures project Manager on staff?

837. How will resource planning be done?

3.2 Change Request: Security Architectures

838. How does a team identify the discrete elements of a configuration?

839. How are changes graded and who is responsible for the rating?

840. What are the duties of the change control team?

841. How are changes requested (forms, method of communication)?

842. Who can suggest changes?

843. Will new change requests be acknowledged in a timely manner?

844. Has your address changed?

845. Are you implementing itil processes?

846. How is quality being addressed on the Security Architectures project?

847. What is the change request log?

848. What are the requirements for urgent changes?

849. Are there requirements attributes that are strongly related to the occurrence of defects and failures?

850. Is it feasible to use requirements attributes as predictors of reliability?

851. When to submit a change request?

852. Which requirements attributes affect the risk to reliability the most?

853. Should a more thorough impact analysis be conducted?

854. How many times must the change be modified or presented to the change control board before it is approved?

855. Who is included in the change control team?

856. Who needs to approve change requests?

857. Since there are no change requests in your Security Architectures project at this point, what must you have before you begin?

3.3 Change Log: Security Architectures

858. Is the requested change request a result of changes in other Security Architectures project(s)?

859. How does this change affect the timeline of the schedule?

860. Will the Security Architectures project fail if the change request is not executed?

861. Who initiated the change request?

862. How does this relate to the standards developed for specific business processes?

863. Is this a mandatory replacement?

864. Is the submitted change a new change or a modification of a previously approved change?

865. Does the suggested change request represent a desired enhancement to the products functionality?

866. Do the described changes impact on the integrity or security of the system?

867. Does the suggested change request seem to represent a necessary enhancement to the product?

868. When was the request submitted?

869. How does this change affect scope?

870. When was the request approved?

871. Is the change backward compatible without limitations?

872. Is the change request within Security Architectures project scope?

873. Is the change request open, closed or pending?

3.4 Decision Log: Security Architectures

874. How do you know when you are achieving it?

875. Do strategies and tactics aimed at less than full control reduce the costs of management or simply shift the cost burden?

876. What alternatives/risks were considered?

877. At what point in time does loss become unacceptable?

878. Who will be given a copy of this document and where will it be kept?

879. How consolidated and comprehensive a story can you tell by capturing currently available incident data in a central location and through a log of key decisions during an incident?

880. How does an increasing emphasis on cost containment influence the strategies and tactics used?

881. Linked to original objective?

882. What is your overall strategy for quality control / quality assurance procedures?

883. What is the average size of your matters in an applicable measurement?

884. Who is the decisionmaker?

885. How does provision of information, both in terms of content and presentation, influence acceptance of alternative strategies?

886. What eDiscovery problem or issue did your organization set out to fix or make better?

887. How does the use a Decision Support System influence the strategies/tactics or costs?

888. What are the cost implications?

889. Does anything need to be adjusted?

890. It becomes critical to track and periodically revisit both operational effectiveness; Are you noticing all that you need to, and are you interpreting what you see effectively?

891. Is everything working as expected?

892. How effective is maintaining the log at facilitating organizational learning?

893. Is your opponent open to a non-traditional workflow, or will it likely challenge anything you do?

3.5 Quality Audit: Security Architectures

894. Are goals well supported with strategies, operational plans, manuals and training?

895. What review processes are in place for your organizations major activities?

896. Are the intentions consistent with external obligations (such as applicable laws)?

897. Are all complaints involving the possible failure of a device, labeling, or packaging to meet any of its specifications reviewed, evaluated, and investigated?

898. How does your organization know that its systems for providing high quality consultancy services to external parties are appropriately effective and constructive?

899. What does an analysis of your organizations staff profile suggest in terms of its planning, and how is this being addressed?

900. How does your organization know that its system for governing staff behaviour is appropriately effective and constructive?

901. How does your organization know that its relationships with other relevant organizations are appropriately effective and constructive?

902. Is progress against the intentions measurable?

903. How does your organization know that its staff placements are appropriately effective and constructive in relation to program-related learning outcomes?

904. How does your organization know that its information technology system is serving its needs as effectively and constructively as is appropriate?

905. How does your organization know that it is appropriately effective and constructive in preparing its staff for organizational aspirations?

906. How does your organization know that its management system is appropriately effective and constructive?

907. How does your organization know that its management of its ethical responsibilities is appropriately effective and constructive?

908. How does your organization know that its methods are appropriately effective and constructive?

909. How does your organization know that the support for its staff is appropriately effective and constructive?

910. Is refuse and garbage adequately stored and disposed of with sufficient frequency to prevent contamination?

911. How does your organization know that its policy management system is appropriately effective and

constructive?

912. Does the supplier use a formal quality system?

913. What are the main things that hinder your ability to do a good job?

3.6 Team Directory: Security Architectures

914. Who is the Sponsor?

915. Contract requirements complied with?

916. Who are the Team Members?

917. What needs to be communicated?

918. Why is the work necessary?

919. Who will report Security Architectures project status to all stakeholders?

920. Do purchase specifications and configurations match requirements?

921. When does information need to be distributed?

922. Process decisions: are contractors adequately prosecuting the work?

923. Process decisions: do job conditions warrant additional actions to collect job information and document on-site activity?

924. How will the team handle changes?

925. How will you accomplish and manage the objectives?

926. Where should the information be distributed?

927. Process decisions: are all start-up, turn over and close out requirements of the contract satisfied?

928. Process decisions: is work progressing on schedule and per contract requirements?

929. Who will talk to the customer?

930. How and in what format should information be presented?

931. Decisions: is the most suitable form of contract being used?

932. Process decisions: do invoice amounts match accepted work in place?

3.7 Team Operating Agreement: Security Architectures

933. What is teaming?

934. What are the boundaries (organizational or geographic) within which you operate?

935. What administrative supports will be put in place to support the team and the teams supervisor?

936. How does teaming fit in with overall organizational goals and meet organizational needs?

937. What is your unique contribution to your organization?

938. Does your team need access to all documents and information at all times?

939. To whom do you deliver your services?

940. Is compensation based on team and individual performance?

941. How will group handle unplanned absences?

942. Do you leverage technology engagement tools group chat, polls, screen sharing, etc.?

943. How will you divide work equitably?

944. What types of accommodations will be

formulated and put in place for sustaining the team?

945. Do you upload presentation materials in advance and test the technology?

946. Do team members reside in more than two countries?

947. Why does your organization want to participate in teaming?

948. Are there influences outside the team that may affect performance, and if so, have you identified and addressed them?

949. Do you determine the meeting length and time of day?

950. Have you established procedures that team members can follow to work effectively together, such as a team operating agreement?

951. Did you determine the technology methods that best match the messages to be communicated?

952. What is group supervision?

3.8 Team Performance Assessment: Security Architectures

953. How do you manage human resources?

954. When does the medium matter?

955. To what degree do all members feel responsible for all agreed-upon measures?

956. To what degree does the teams purpose constitute a broader, deeper aspiration than just accomplishing short-term goals?

957. To what degree will team members, individually and collectively, commit time to help themselves and others learn and develop skills?

958. To what degree can the team measure progress against specific goals?

959. To what degree do members articulate the goals beyond the team membership?

960. What are teams?

961. Can team performance be reliably measured in simulator and live exercises using the same assessment tool?

962. To what degree are the goals realistic?

963. To what degree is there a sense that only the

team can succeed?

964. If you are worried about method variance before you collect data, what sort of design elements might you include to reduce or eliminate the threat of method variance?

965. To what degree do team members articulate the teams work approach?

966. To what degree does the teams purpose contain themes that are particularly meaningful and memorable?

967. How do you recognize and praise members for contributions?

968. To what degree can team members meet frequently enough to accomplish the teams ends?

969. To what degree does the team possess adequate membership to achieve its ends?

970. To what degree is the team cognizant of small wins to be celebrated along the way?

971. To what degree do team members understand one anothers roles and skills?

972. To what degree will the team adopt a concrete, clearly understood, and agreed-upon approach that will result in achievement of the teams goals?

3.9 Team Member Performance Assessment: Security Architectures

973. How do you make use of research?

974. Are any governance changes sufficient to impact achievement?

975. How do you implement Cost Reduction?

976. How do you create a self-sustaining capacity for a collaborative culture?

977. Can your organization rate by exception and assume that most employees are performing at an acceptable level?

978. What are the standards or expectations for success?

979. What, if any, steps are available for employees who feel they have been unfairly or inaccurately rated?

980. In what areas would you like to concentrate your knowledge and resources?

981. What kinds of performance factors / elements do you use?

982. How do you determine which data are the most important to use, analyze, or review?

983. Did training work?

984. What is the Business Management Oversight Process?

985. What are top priorities?

986. How accurately is your plan implemented?

987. To what degree are the teams goals and objectives clear, simple, and measurable?

988. How should adaptive assessments be implemented?

3.10 Issue Log: Security Architectures

989. Is access to the Issue Log controlled?

990. Why multiple evaluators?

991. Why do you manage human resources?

992. What is the status of the issue?

993. What help do you and your team need from the stakeholders?

994. In classifying stakeholders, which approach to do so are you using?

995. Is the issue log kept in a safe place?

996. How were past initiatives successful?

997. Which stakeholders are thought leaders, influences, or early adopters?

998. What approaches to you feel are the best ones to use?

999. What is the impact on the Business Case?

1000. Who do you turn to if you have questions?

1001. Persistence; will users learn a work around or will they be bothered every time?

4.0 Monitoring and Controlling Process Group: Security Architectures

1002. Are there areas that need improvement?

1003. How to ensure validity, quality and consistency?

1004. Did the Security Architectures project team have the right skills?

1005. What are the goals of the program?

1006. Propriety: who needs to be involved in the evaluation to be ethical?

1007. How were collaborations developed, and how are they sustained?

1008. Just how important is your work to the overall success of the Security Architectures project?

1009. Who needs to be involved in the planning?

1010. What is the timeline?

1011. Is the program in place as intended?

1012. Have operating capacities been created and/or reinforced in partners?

1013. Is the verbiage used appropriate and understandable?

1014. User: who wants the information and what are they interested in?

1015. How can you monitor progress?

1016. How is Agile Security Architectures project Management done?

4.1 Project Performance Report: Security Architectures

1017. To what degree do the relationships of the informal organization motivate taskrelevant behavior and facilitate task completion?

1018. To what degree are the demands of the task compatible with and converge with the relationships of the informal organization?

1019. What is the degree to which rules govern information exchange between groups?

1020. To what degree are the demands of the task compatible with and converge with the mission and functions of the formal organization?

1021. What degree are the relative importance and priority of the goals clear to all team members?

1022. To what degree is the information network consistent with the structure of the formal organization?

1023. To what degree does the teams work approach provide opportunity for members to engage in results-based evaluation?

1024. To what degree are the members clear on what they are individually responsible for and what they are jointly responsible for?

1025. To what degree will new and supplemental skills be introduced as the need is recognized?

1026. To what degree can all members engage in open and interactive considerations?

1027. How is the data used?

1028. To what degree does the teams work approach provide opportunity for members to engage in open interaction?

1029. To what degree do individual skills and abilities match task demands?

4.2 Variance Analysis: Security Architectures

1030. Are the bases and rates for allocating costs from each indirect pool consistently applied?

1031. Are management actions taken to reduce indirect costs when there are significant adverse variances?

1032. What is the budgeted cost for work scheduled?

1033. How does your organization measure performance?

1034. What costs are avoidable if one or more customers are dropped?

1035. Are the actual costs used for variance analysis reconcilable with data from the accounting system?

1036. Can the contractor substantiate work package and planning package budgets?

1037. Are indirect costs charged to the appropriate indirect pools and incurring organization?

1038. Does the contractors system include procedures for measuring the performance of critical subcontractors?

1039. What is the dollar amount of the fluctuation?

1040. How does your organization allocate the cost of shared expenses and services?

1041. At what point should variances be isolated and brought to the attention of the management?

1042. How do you identify potential or actual overruns and underruns?

1043. Are all budgets assigned to control accounts?

1044. Are there changes in the direct base to which overhead costs are allocated?

1045. Does the contractors system identify work accomplishment against the schedule plan?

1046. How do you manage changes in the nature of the overhead requirements?

1047. Favorable or unfavorable variance?

4.3 Earned Value Status: Security Architectures

1048. Earned value can be used in almost any Security Architectures project situation and in almost any Security Architectures project environment. it may be used on large Security Architectures projects, medium sized Security Architectures projects, tiny Security Architectures projects (in cut-down form), complex and simple Security Architectures projects and in any market sector. some people, of course, know all about earned value, they have used it for years - but perhaps not as effectively as they could have?

1049. How much is it going to cost by the finish?

1050. Where are your problem areas?

1051. Verification is a process of ensuring that the developed system satisfies the stakeholders agreements and specifications; Are you building the product right? What do you verify?

1052. Are you hitting your Security Architectures projects targets?

1053. What is the unit of forecast value?

1054. Validation is a process of ensuring that the developed system will actually achieve the stakeholders desired outcomes; Are you building the right product? What do you validate?

1055. Where is evidence-based earned value in your organization reported?

1056. When is it going to finish?

1057. How does this compare with other Security Architectures projects?

1058. If earned value management (EVM) is so good in determining the true status of a Security Architectures project and Security Architectures project its completion, why is it that hardly any one uses it in information systems related Security Architectures projects?

4.4 Risk Audit: Security Architectures

1059. Are tools for analysis and design available?

1060. If applicable; are compilers and code generators available and suitable for the product to be built?

1061. Risks with Security Architectures projects or new initiatives?

1062. Have all possible risks/hazards been identified (including injury to staff, damage to equipment, impact on others in the community)?

1063. Do you have an understanding of insurance claims processes?

1064. Is the customer willing to participate in reviews?

1065. Is all required equipment available?

1066. What are the commonly used work arounds in high risk areas?

1067. Does your organization have a social media policy and procedure?

1068. Are you aware of the industry standards that apply to your operations?

1069. Are the software tools integrated with each other?

1070. To what extent are auditors effective at linking

business risks and management assertions?

1071. When your organization is entering into a major contract, does it seek legal advice?

1072. How are risk appetites expressed?

1073. What can be measured?

1074. Are staff committed for the duration of the product?

1075. Strategic business risk audit methodologies; are corresponding an attempt to sell other services, and is management becoming the client of the audit rather than the shareholder?

1076. Do end-users have realistic expectations?

1077. Do you have a consistent repeatable process that is actually used?

1078. What responsibilities for quality, errors, and outcomes have been delegated to staff (or others) without adequate oversight?

4.5 Contractor Status Report: Security Architectures

1079. What was the budget or estimated cost for your organizations services?

1080. Are there contractual transfer concerns?

1081. How is risk transferred?

1082. What is the average response time for answering a support call?

1083. What are the minimum and optimal bandwidth requirements for the proposed solution?

1084. Describe how often regular updates are made to the proposed solution. Are corresponding regular updates included in the standard maintenance plan?

1085. How does the proposed individual meet each requirement?

1086. Who can list a Security Architectures project as organization experience, your organization or a previous employee of your organization?

1087. What process manages the contracts?

1088. What was the actual budget or estimated cost for your organizations services?

1089. What was the final actual cost?

1090. How long have you been using the services?

1091. What was the overall budget or estimated cost?

1092. If applicable; describe your standard schedule for new software version releases. Are new software version releases included in the standard maintenance plan?

4.6 Formal Acceptance: Security Architectures

1093. Was business value realized?

1094. What is the Acceptance Management Process?

1095. What features, practices, and processes proved to be strengths or weaknesses?

1096. Who supplies data?

1097. Do you buy pre-configured systems or build your own configuration?

1098. Does it do what Security Architectures project team said it would?

1099. General estimate of the costs and times to complete the Security Architectures project?

1100. Who would use it?

1101. Was the client satisfied with the Security Architectures project results?

1102. Do you perform formal acceptance or burn-in tests?

1103. What are the requirements against which to test, Who will execute?

1104. Does it do what client said it would?

1105. What function(s) does it fill or meet?

1106. Was the Security Architectures project managed well?

1107. Is formal acceptance of the Security Architectures project product documented and distributed?

1108. What can you do better next time?

1109. How well did the team follow the methodology?

1110. What lessons were learned about your Security Architectures project management methodology?

1111. Was the Security Architectures project work done on time, within budget, and according to specification?

1112. Did the Security Architectures project manager and team act in a professional and ethical manner?

5.0 Closing Process Group: Security Architectures

1113. What areas were overlooked on this Security Architectures project?

1114. Did the Security Architectures project team have the right skills?

1115. Specific - is the objective clear in terms of what, how, when, and where the situation will be changed?

1116. How will you know you did it?

1117. What were the desired outcomes?

1118. What is the amount of funding and what Security Architectures project phases are funded?

1119. What can you do better next time, and what specific actions can you take to improve?

1120. Was the schedule met?

1121. How well did you do?

1122. What areas does the group agree are the biggest success on the Security Architectures project?

5.1 Procurement Audit: Security Architectures

1123. Is the procurement process fully digitalized?

1124. What are the required standards of quality assurance or environmental management?

1125. Is there a form specified for bids?

1126. Are approvals needed if changes are made in the quantity or specification of the original purchase requisition?

1127. Were additional works charged at the unit prices agreed in the initial contract?

1128. Is there no evidence that the expert has influenced the decisions taken by the public authority in his/her interest or in the interest of a specific contractor?

1129. Are the internal control systems operational?

1130. Are there appropriate controls in place to ensure that procurement complies with the relevant legislation?

1131. Is your organization policy on purchasing covered by a written manual?

1132. Is there no evidence of favouritism towards a particular contractor during the evaluation and negotiation processes?

1133. Does the approval include approval of prices?

1134. Are there systems for recording and monitoring in order to discover malpractice and fraud in the procurement function/unit?

1135. Is it clear which procurement procedure your organization has opted for?

1136. Are behaviour modification applied to change procurement of goods and services if procurement is not functioning properly?

1137. Is a risk evaluation performed?

1138. Has the department identified and described the different elements in the procurement process?

1139. Did the conditions included in the contract protect the risk of non-performance by the supplier and were there no conflicting provisions?

1140. Are advantages and disadvantages of in-house production, outsourcing and Public Private Partnerships considered?

1141. Are review meetings organized during contract execution and do they meet demand?

1142. Was the estimated contract value in line with the final cost of the contract awarded?

5.2 Contract Close-Out: Security Architectures

1143. What happens to the recipient of services?

1144. Parties: who is involved?

1145. Parties: Authorized?

1146. Was the contract sufficiently clear so as not to result in numerous disputes and misunderstandings?

1147. Was the contract complete without requiring numerous changes and revisions?

1148. Change in knowledge?

1149. Was the contract type appropriate?

1150. Have all contracts been closed?

1151. How/when used ?

1152. Change in attitude or behavior?

1153. Are the signers the authorized officials?

1154. Have all acceptance criteria been met prior to final payment to contractors?

1155. Change in circumstances?

1156. Has each contract been audited to verify

acceptance and delivery?

1157. Have all contracts been completed?

1158. How does it work?

1159. What is capture management?

1160. Have all contract records been included in the Security Architectures project archives?

1161. Why Outsource?

1162. How is the contracting office notified of the automatic contract close-out?

5.3 Project or Phase Close-Out: Security Architectures

1163. What security considerations needed to be addressed during the procurement life cycle?

1164. Complete yes or no?

1165. Were risks identified and mitigated?

1166. Did the delivered product meet the specified requirements and goals of the Security Architectures project?

1167. What was expected from each stakeholder?

1168. Were the outcomes different from the already stated planned?

1169. What are the mandatory communication needs for each stakeholder?

1170. What is a Risk?

1171. What was the preferred delivery mechanism?

1172. In preparing the Lessons Learned report, should it reflect a consensus viewpoint, or should the report reflect the different individual viewpoints?

1173. What is this stakeholder expecting?

1174. What could be done to improve the process?

1175. What were the actual outcomes?

1176. What is the information level of detail required for each stakeholder?

1177. How much influence did the stakeholder have over others?

1178. Who controlled key decisions that were made?

1179. What process was planned for managing issues/ risks?

1180. Planned completion date?

5.4 Lessons Learned: Security Architectures

1181. Can the lesson learned be replicated?

1182. Were the aims and objectives achieved?

1183. How effective was the documentation that you received with the Security Architectures project product/service?

1184. Was the Security Architectures project manager sufficiently experienced, skilled, trained, supported?

1185. How efficient were Security Architectures project team meetings conducted?

1186. What are the skills directly related to the task?

1187. How effective was Security Architectures project Team member training?

1188. What could have been improved?

1189. How satisfied are you with your involvement in the development and/or review of the Security Architectures project Scope during Security Architectures project Initiation and Planning?

1190. What was the geopolitical history during the origin of your organization and at the time of task input?

1191. Are the lessons more complex and multivariate?

1192. How objective was the collection of data?

1193. What are the conceptual limits of the research?

1194. What were the key issues?

1195. What worked well/did not work well?

1196. What are the internal dependencies?

1197. Are there any data that you have overlooked in identifying lessons?

1198. What were the challenges and pitfalls?

1199. Recommendation: what do you recommend should be done to ensure that others throughout your organization can benefit from what you have learned?

1200. How to write up the lesson identified – how will you document the results of your analysis corresponding that you have an li ready to take the next step in the ll process?

Index

CPSIA information can be obtained
at www.ICGtesting.com
Printed in the USA
BVHW041052100719
553067BV00013B/533/P

9 780655 809449